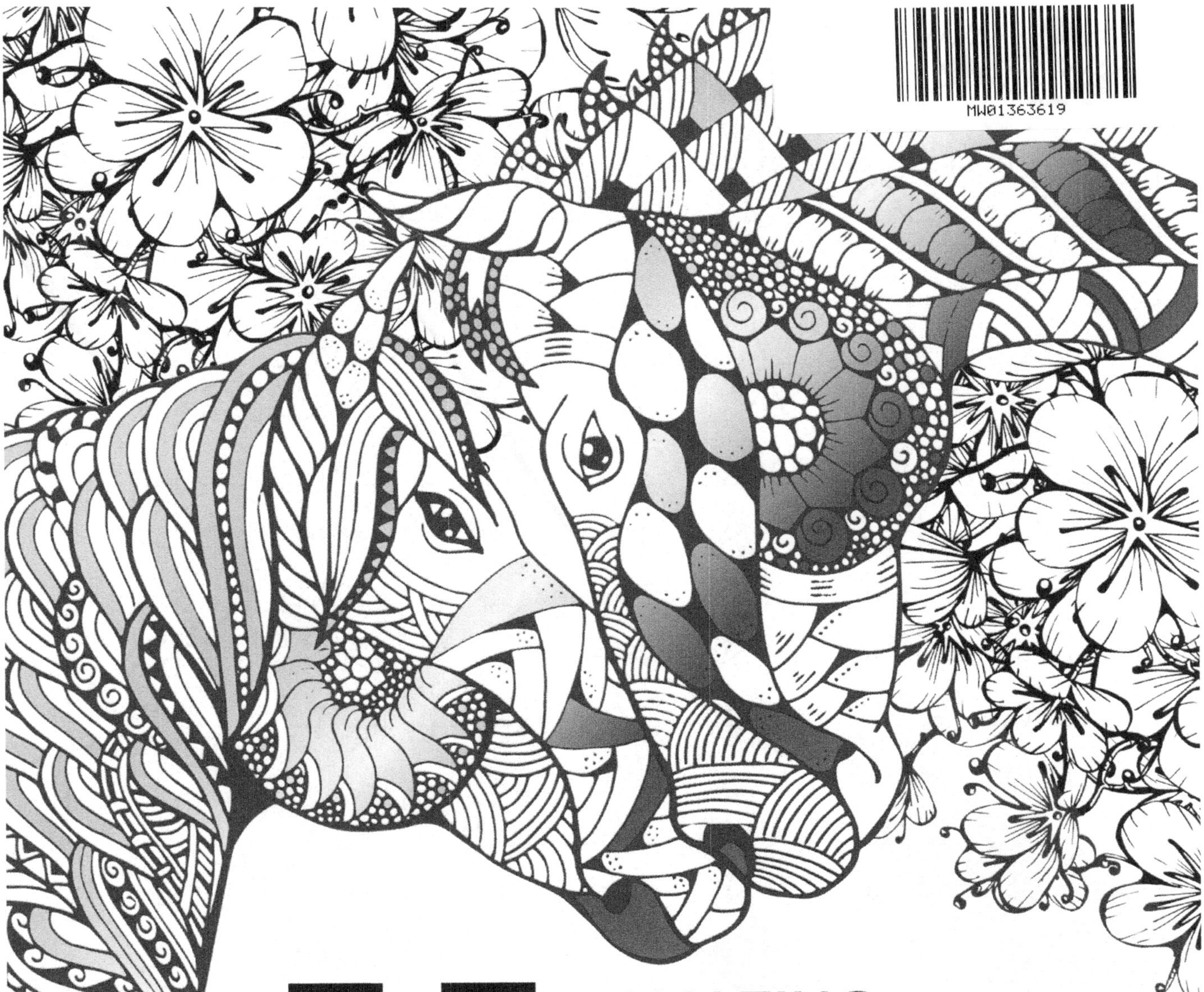

AMAZING HORSE

COLORING BOOKS FOR ADULTS

WONDERFUL DESINGS
AND STRESS RELIEVING PATTERNS

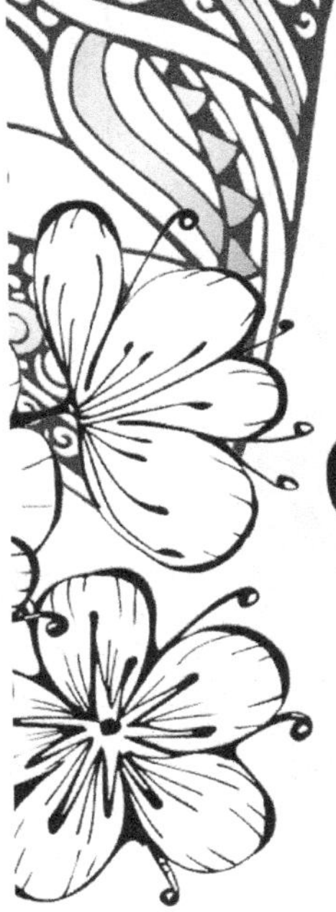

TEST YOUR COLOR

TEST YOUR COLOR

1.

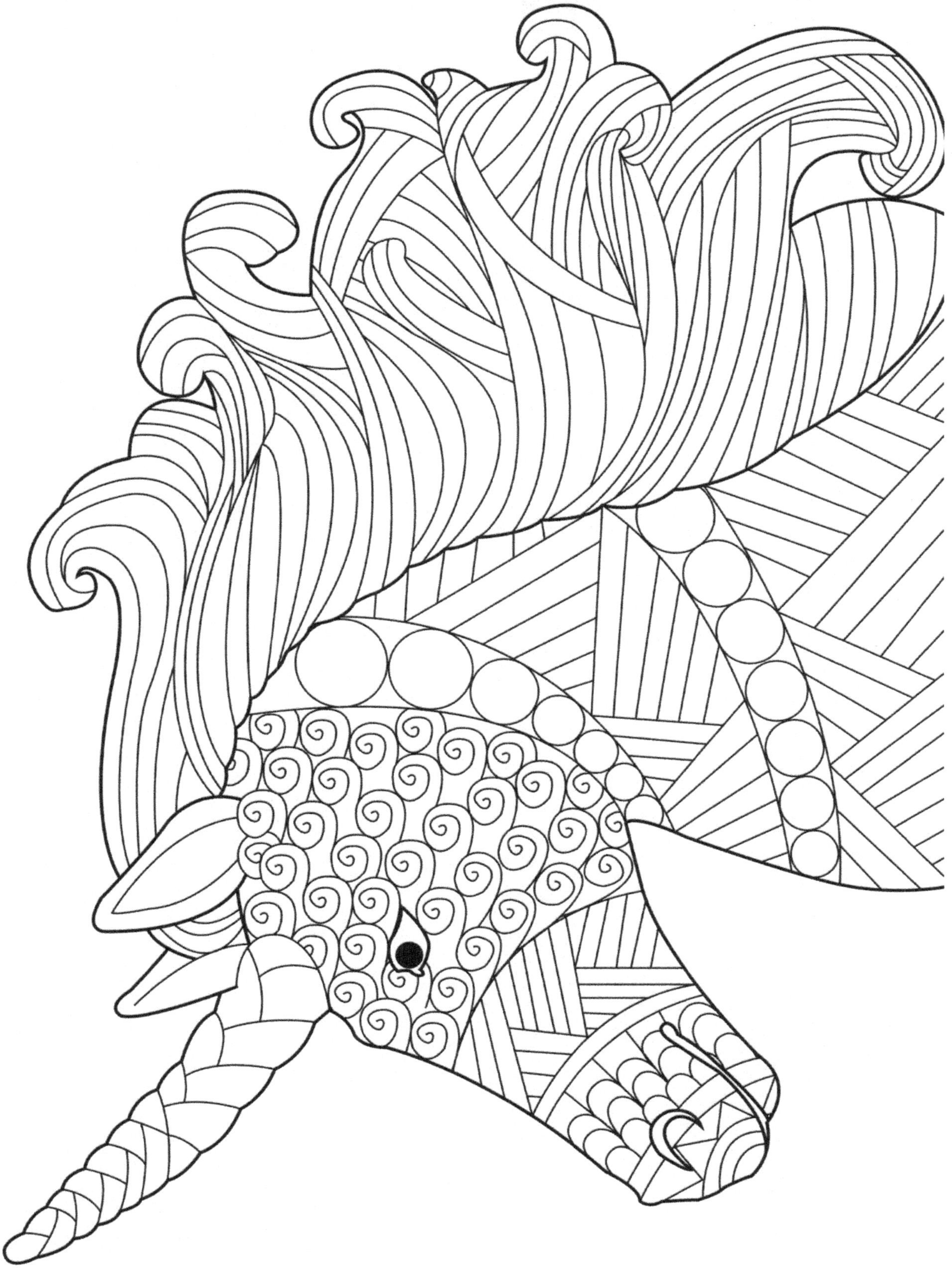

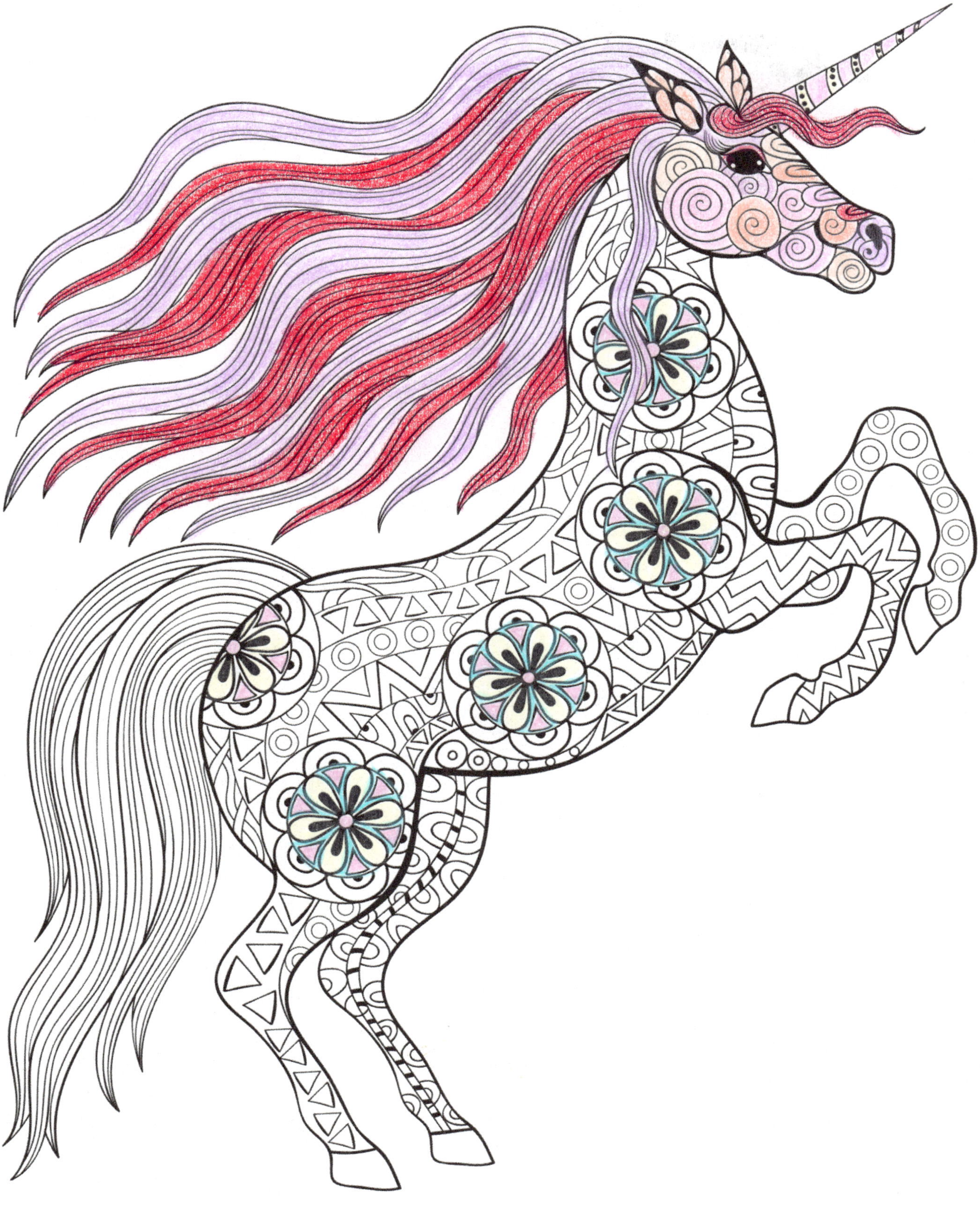

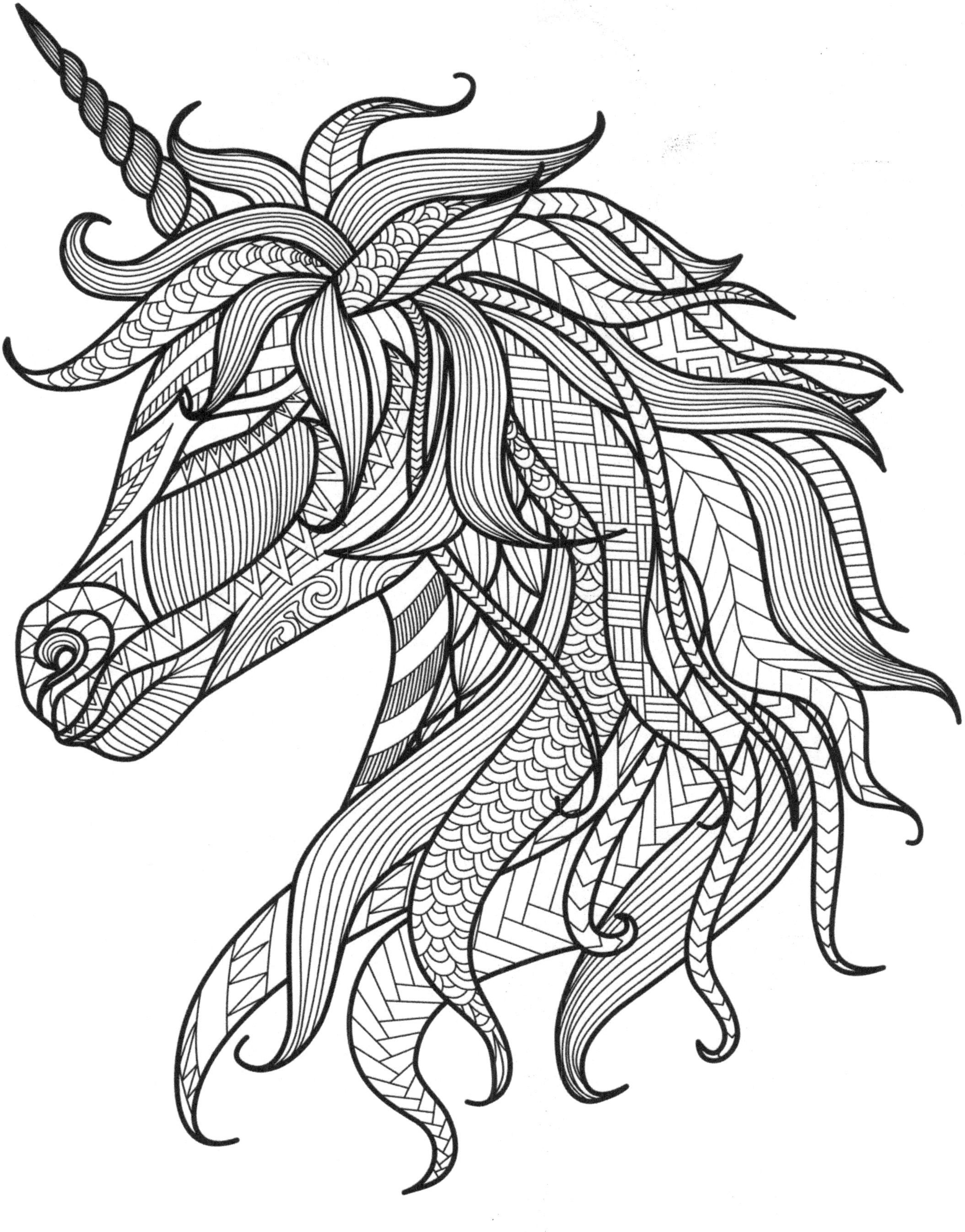

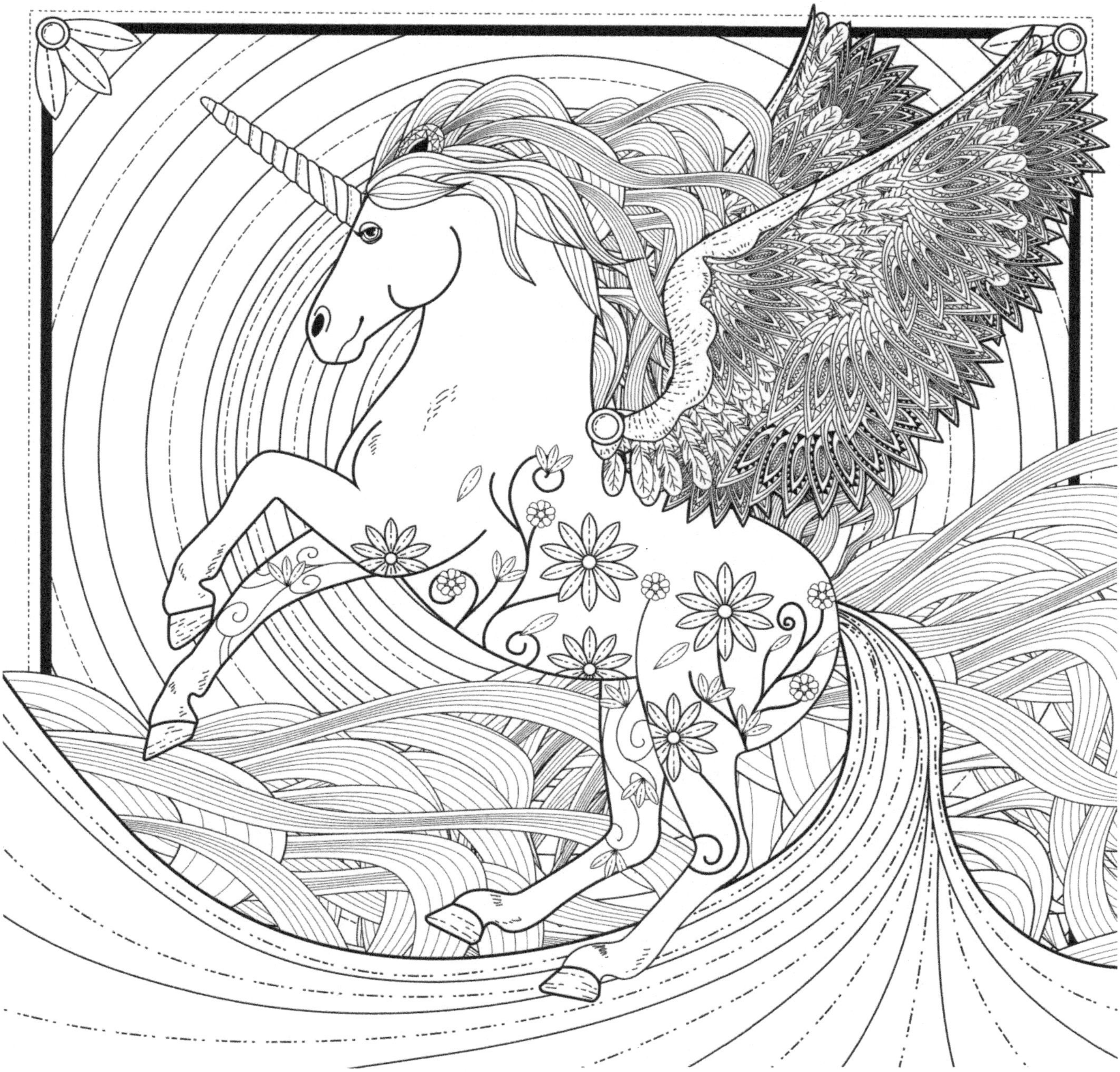

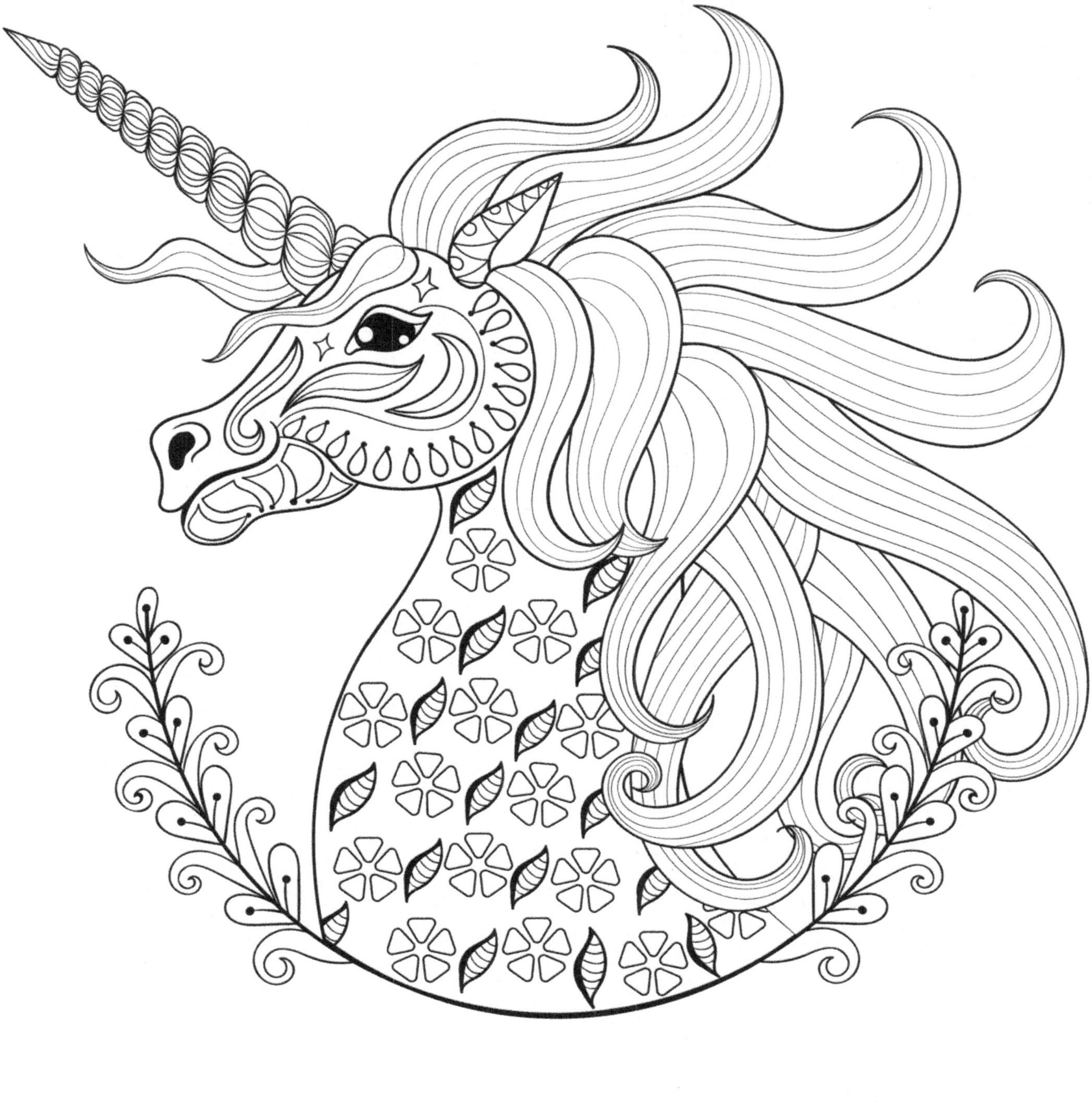

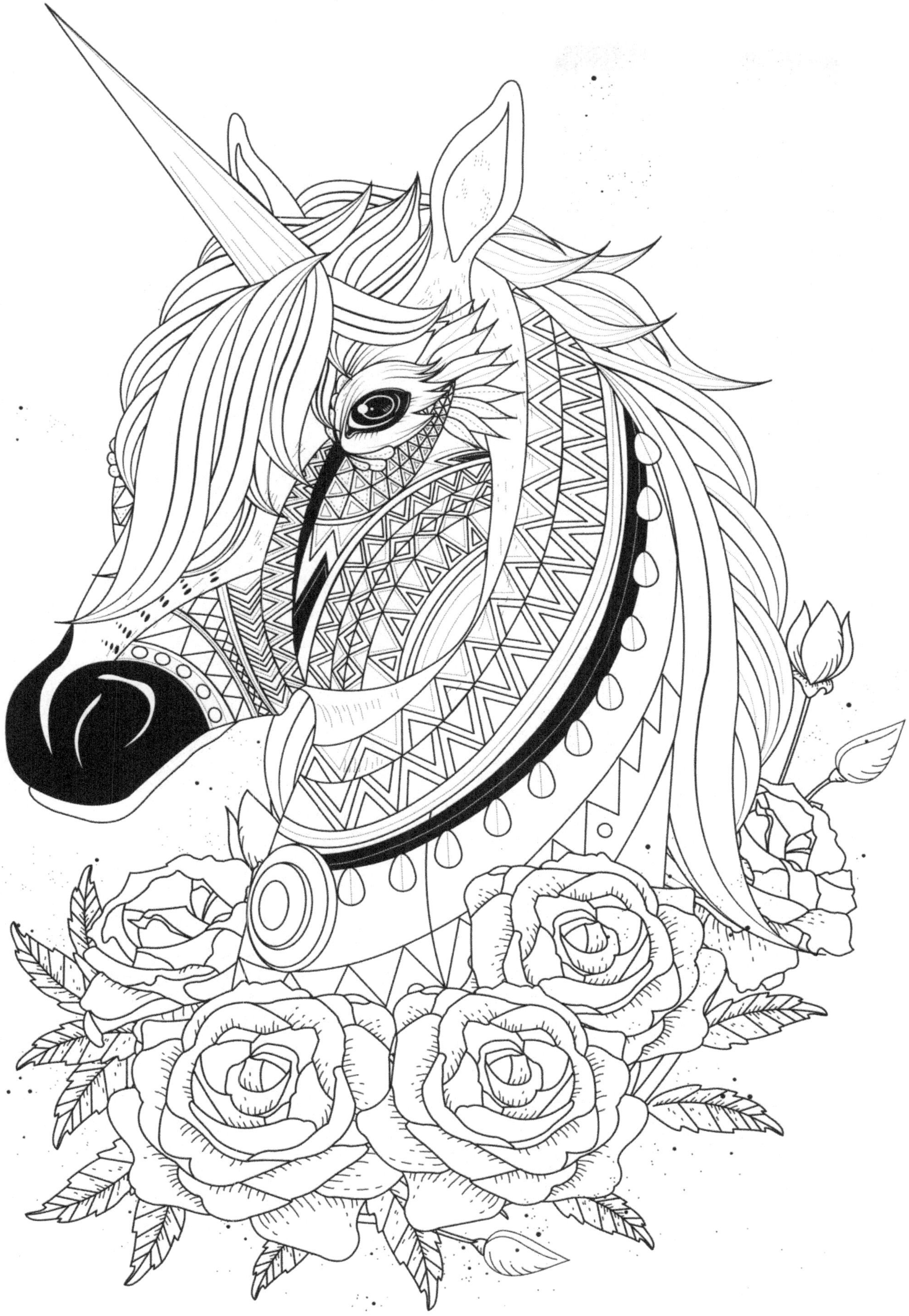

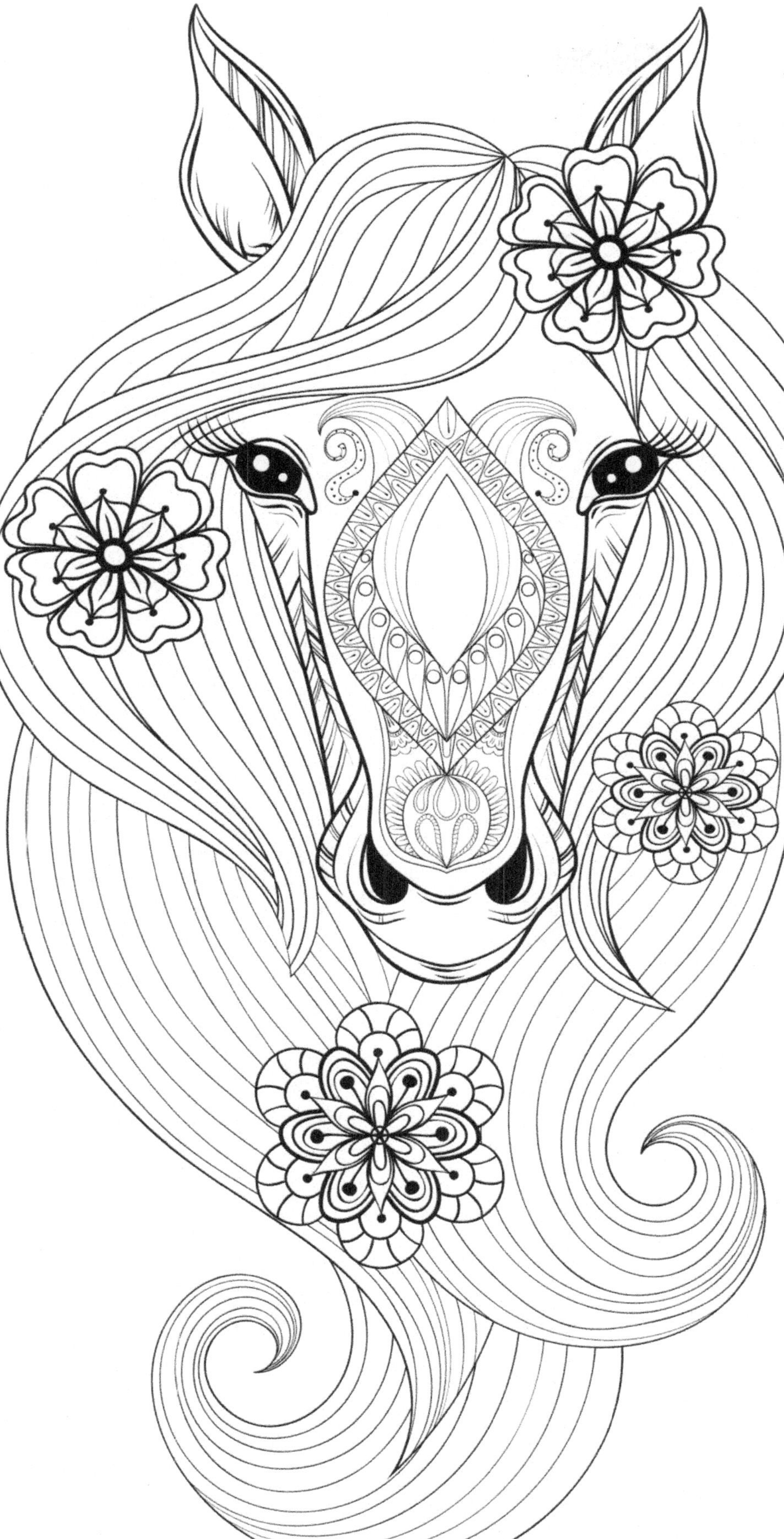

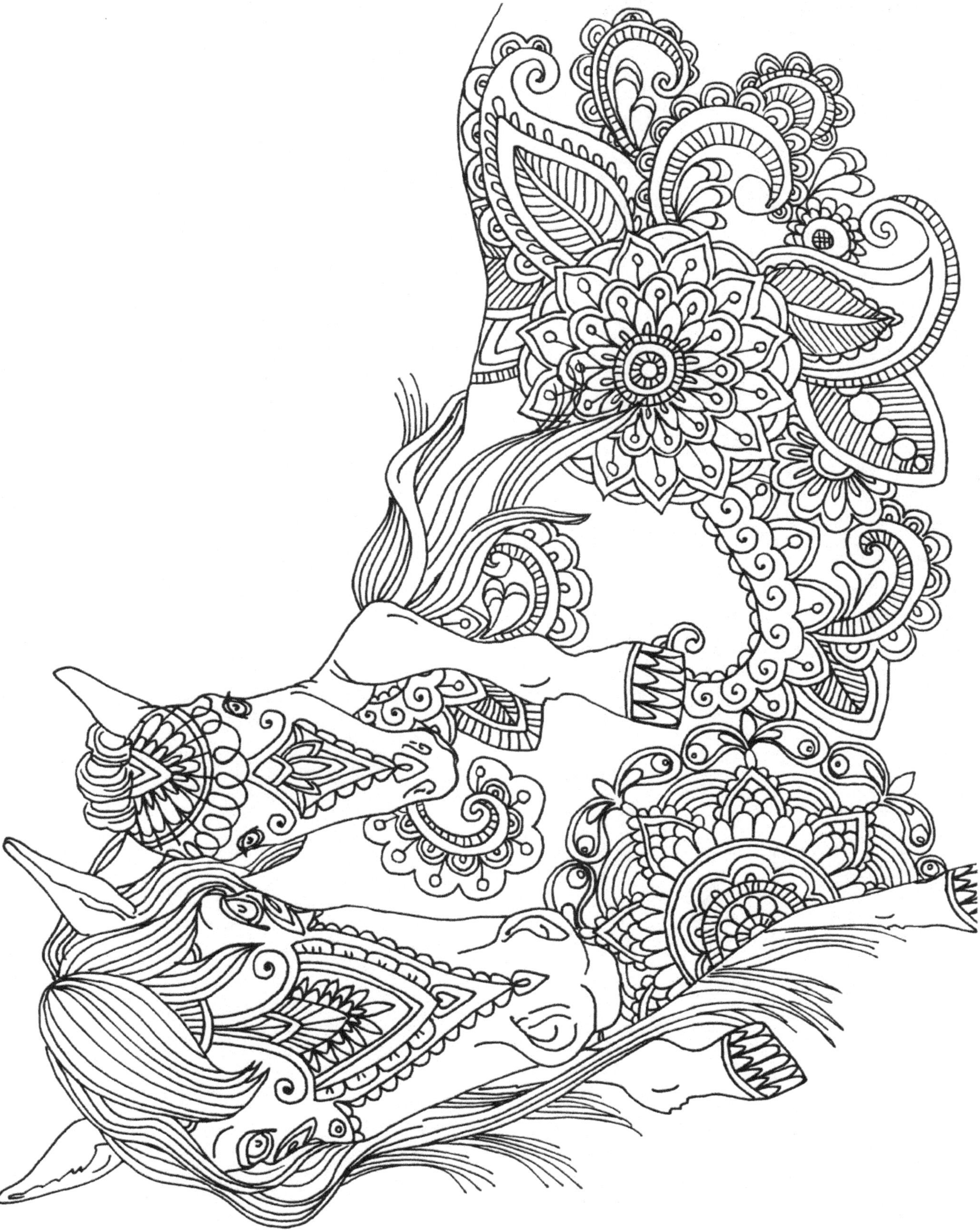

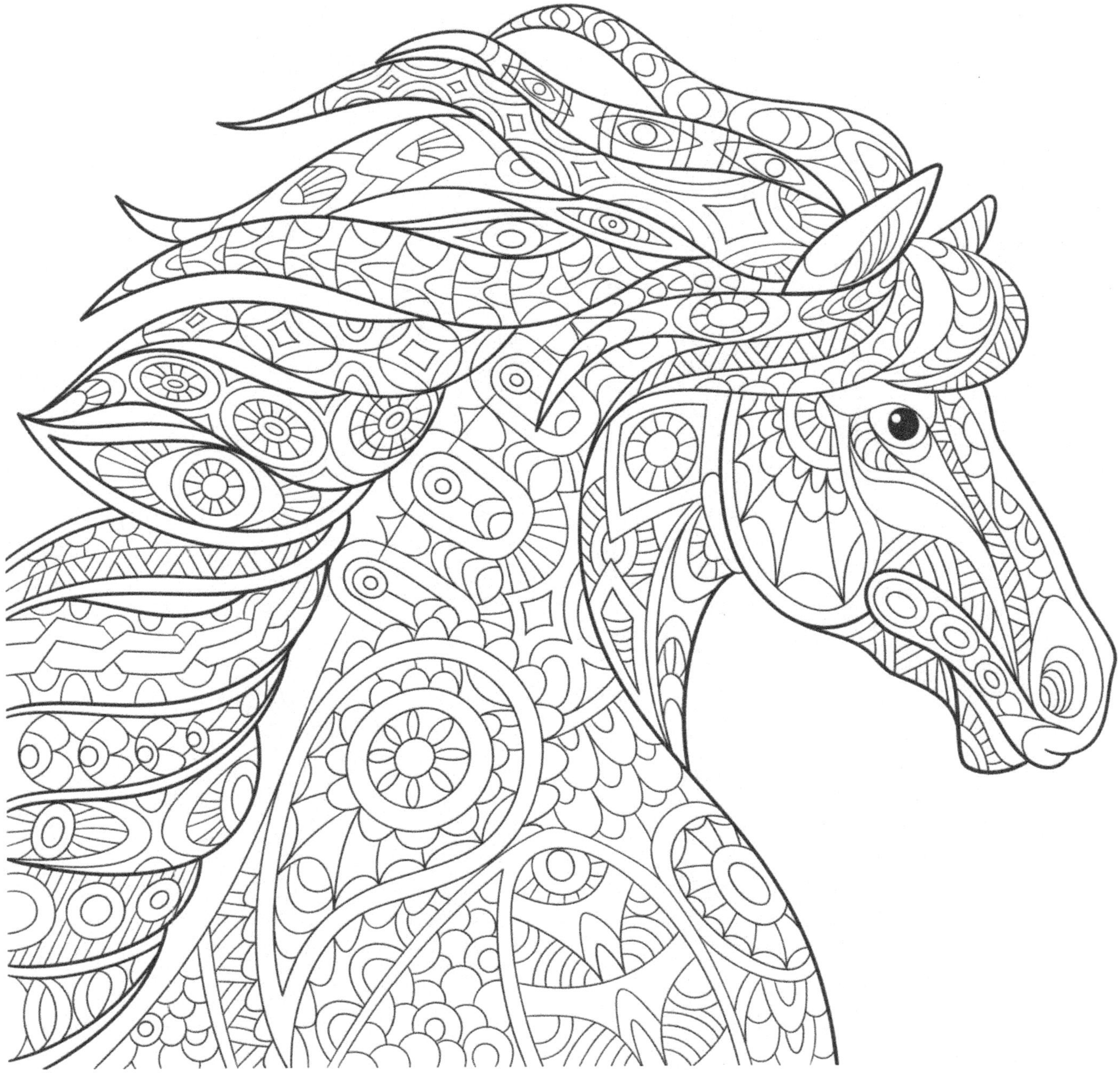

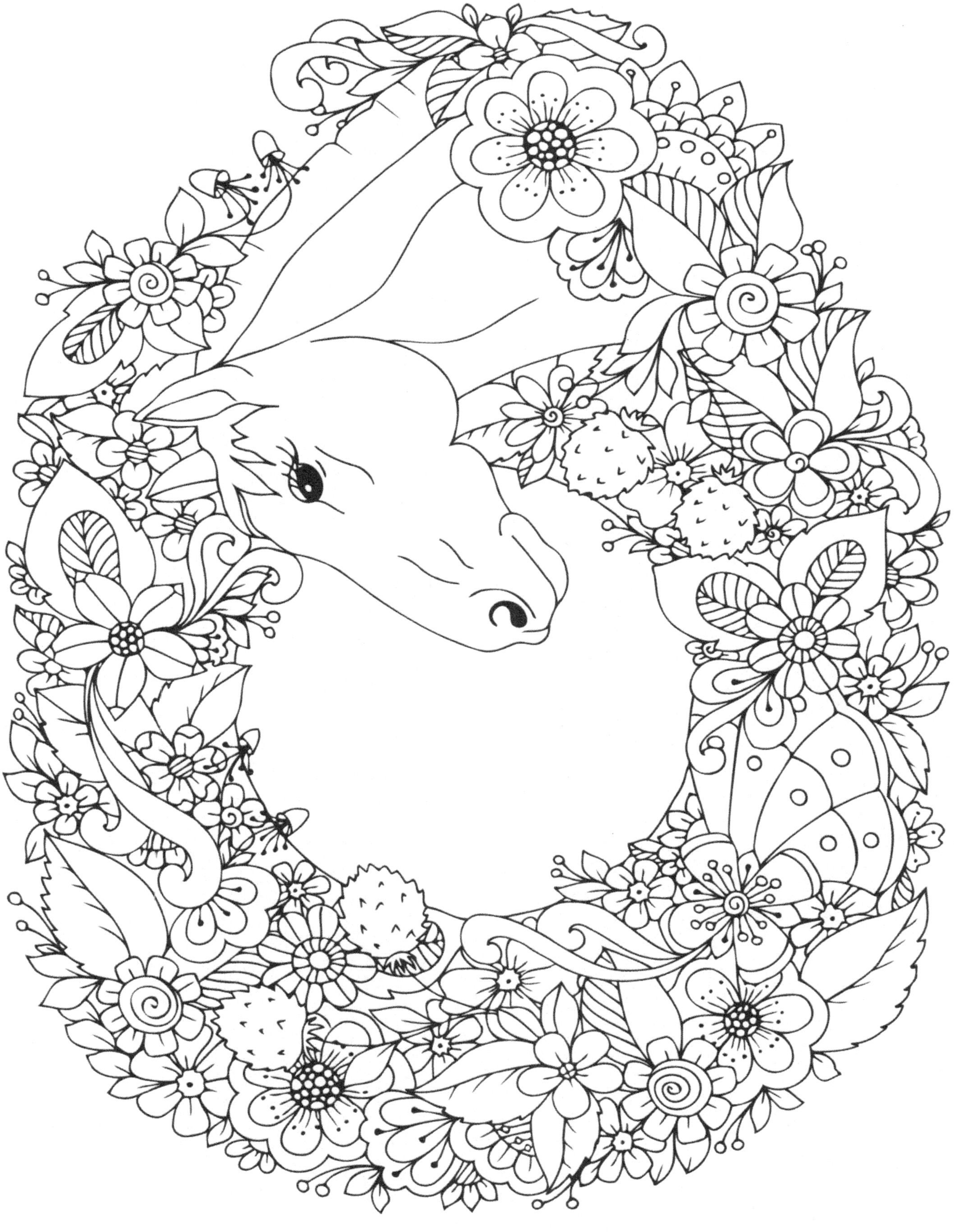

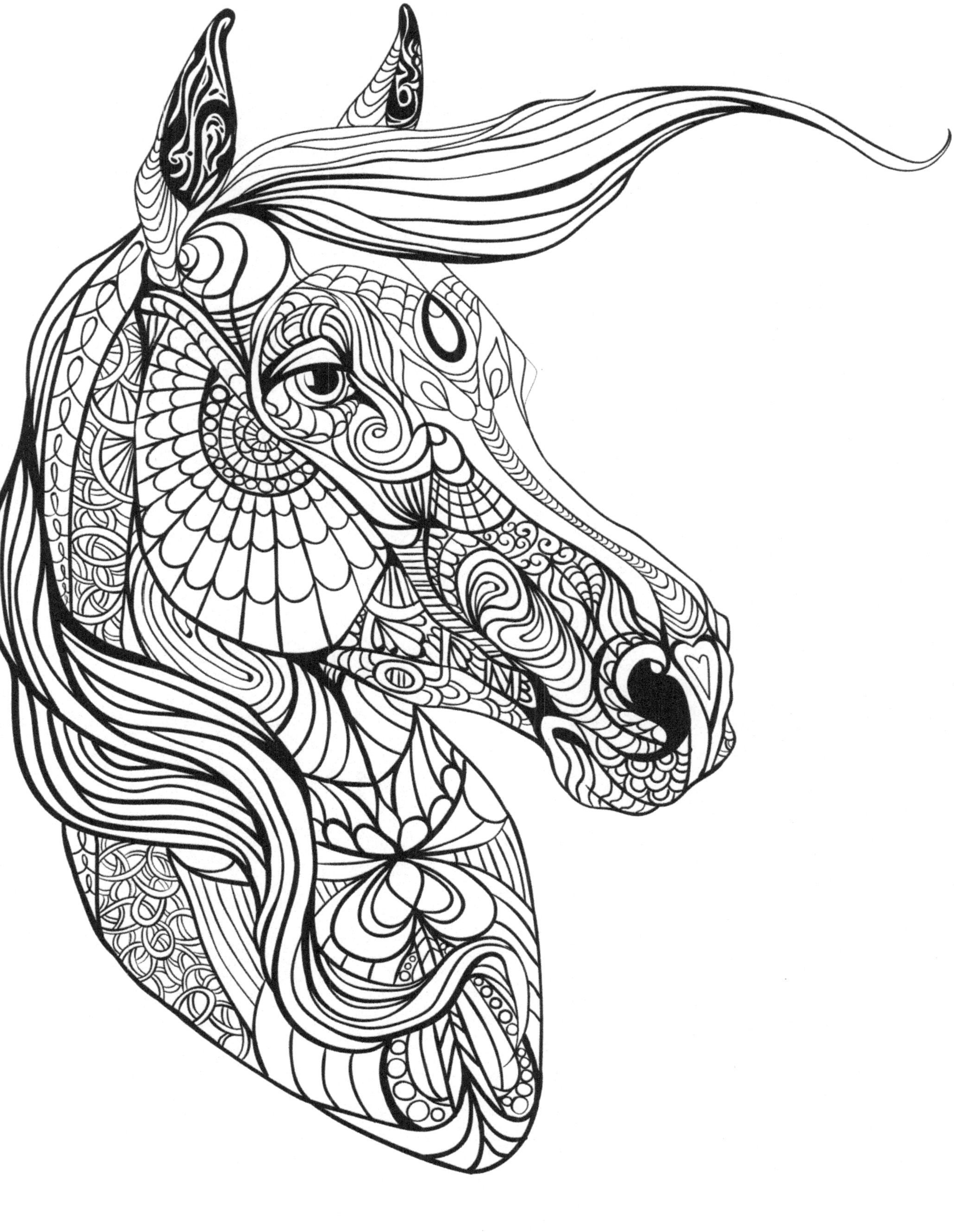

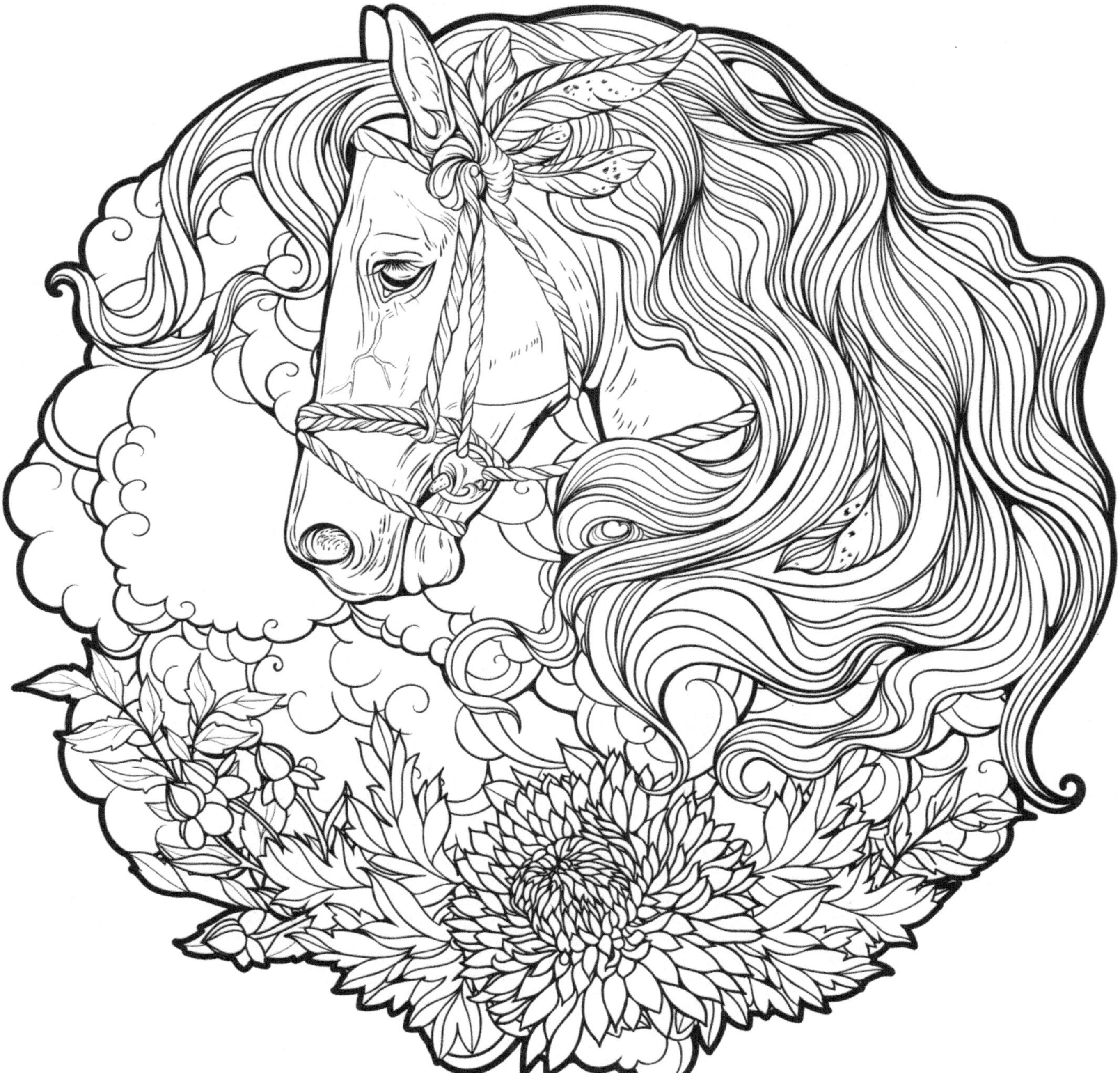

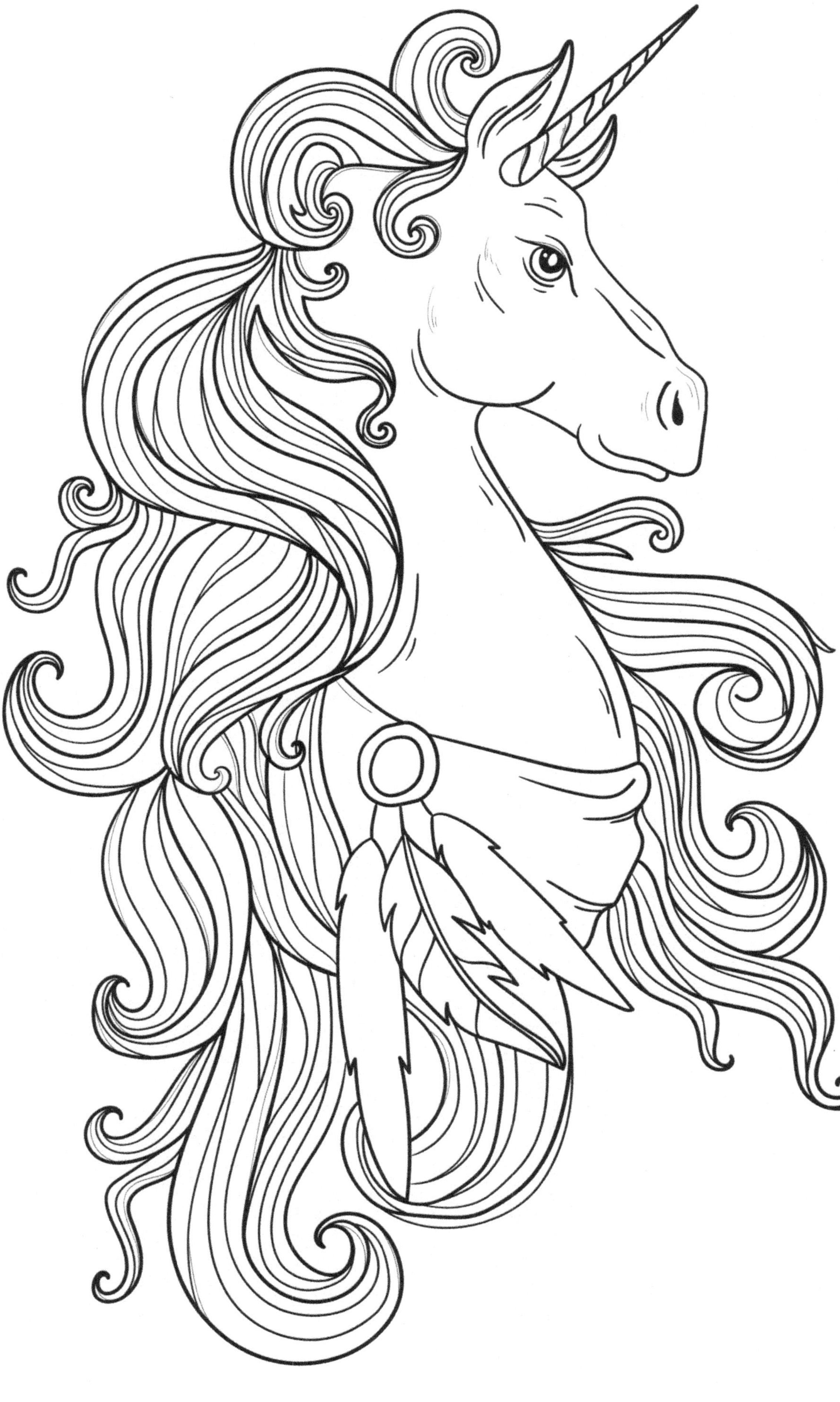

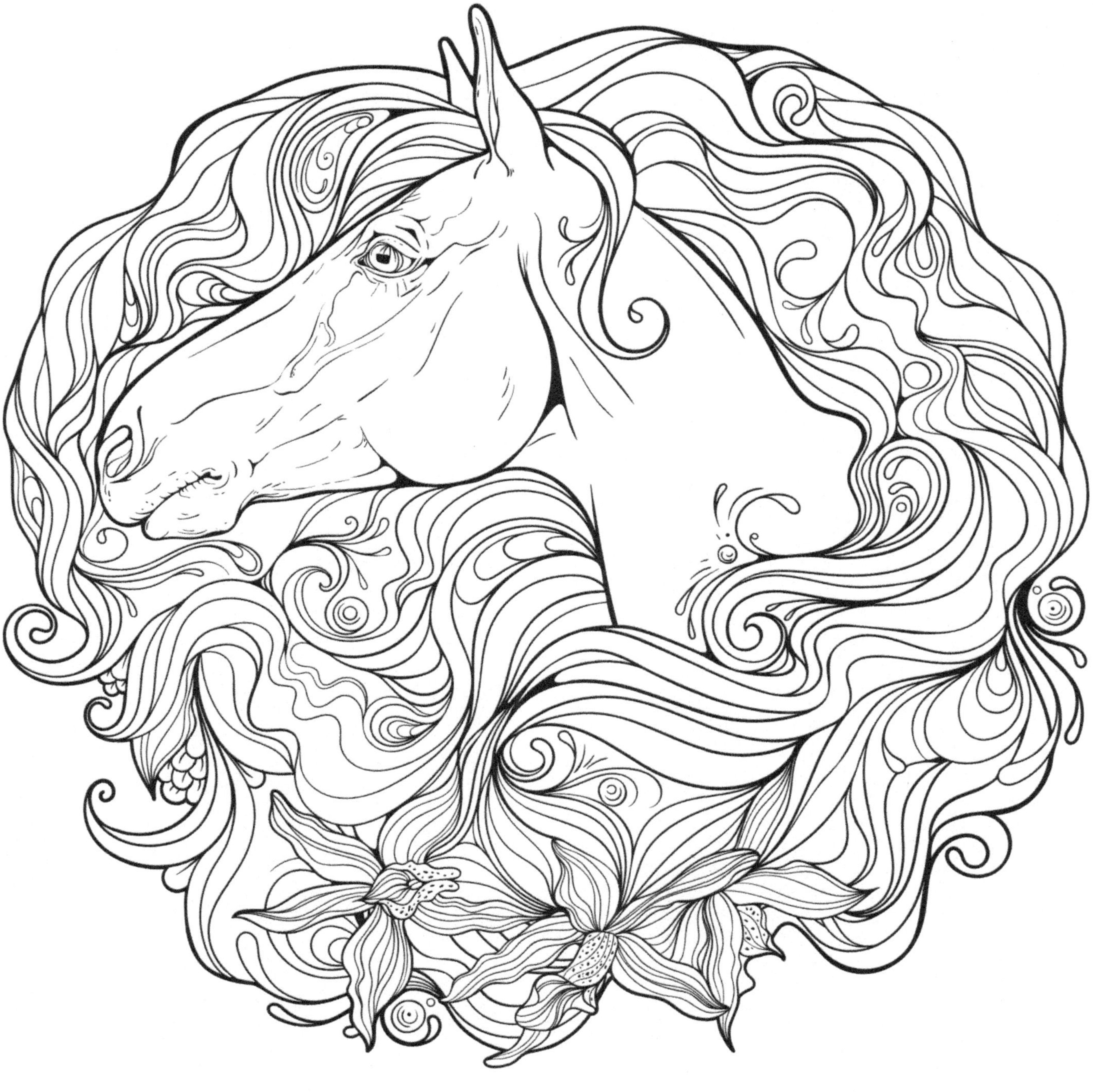

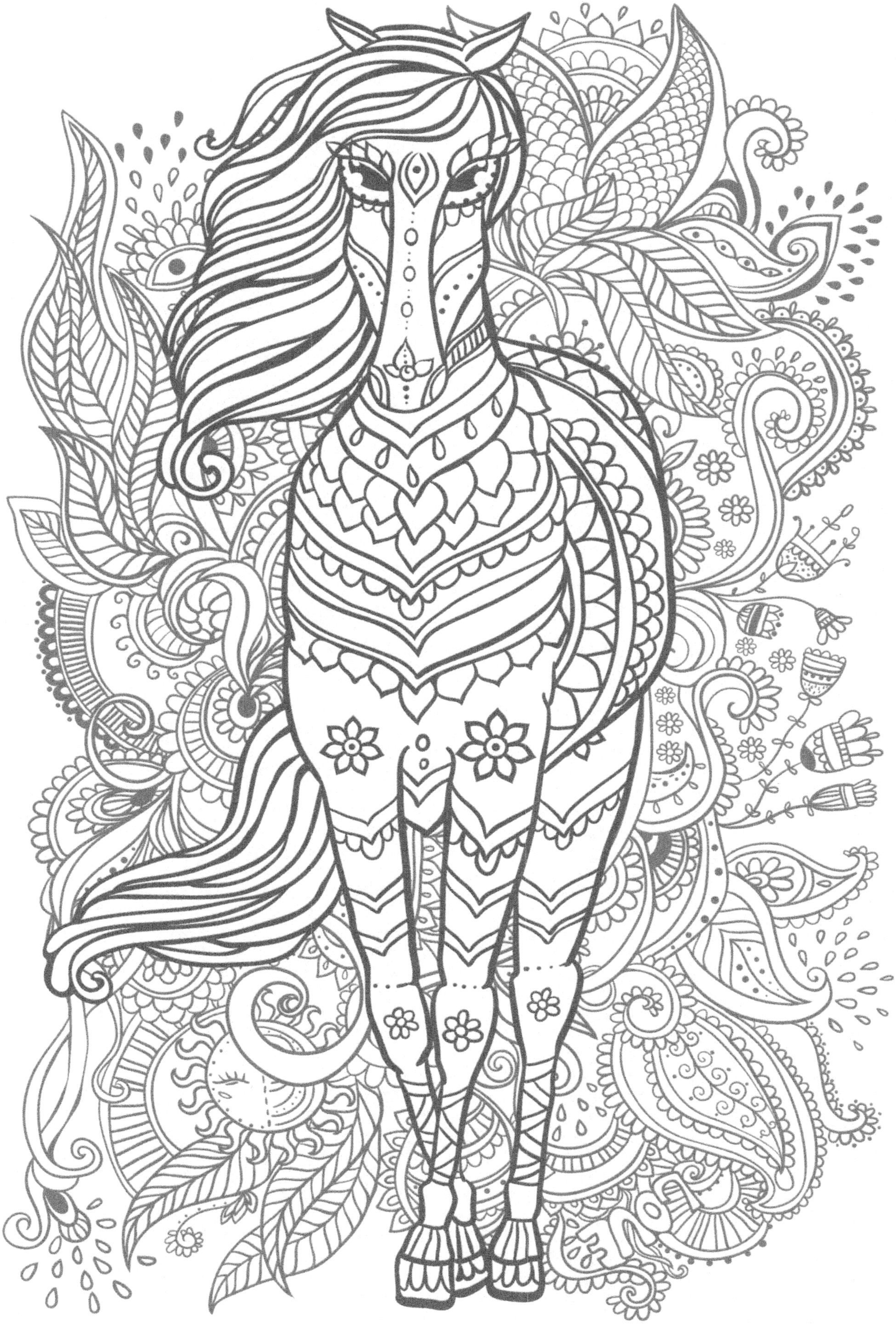

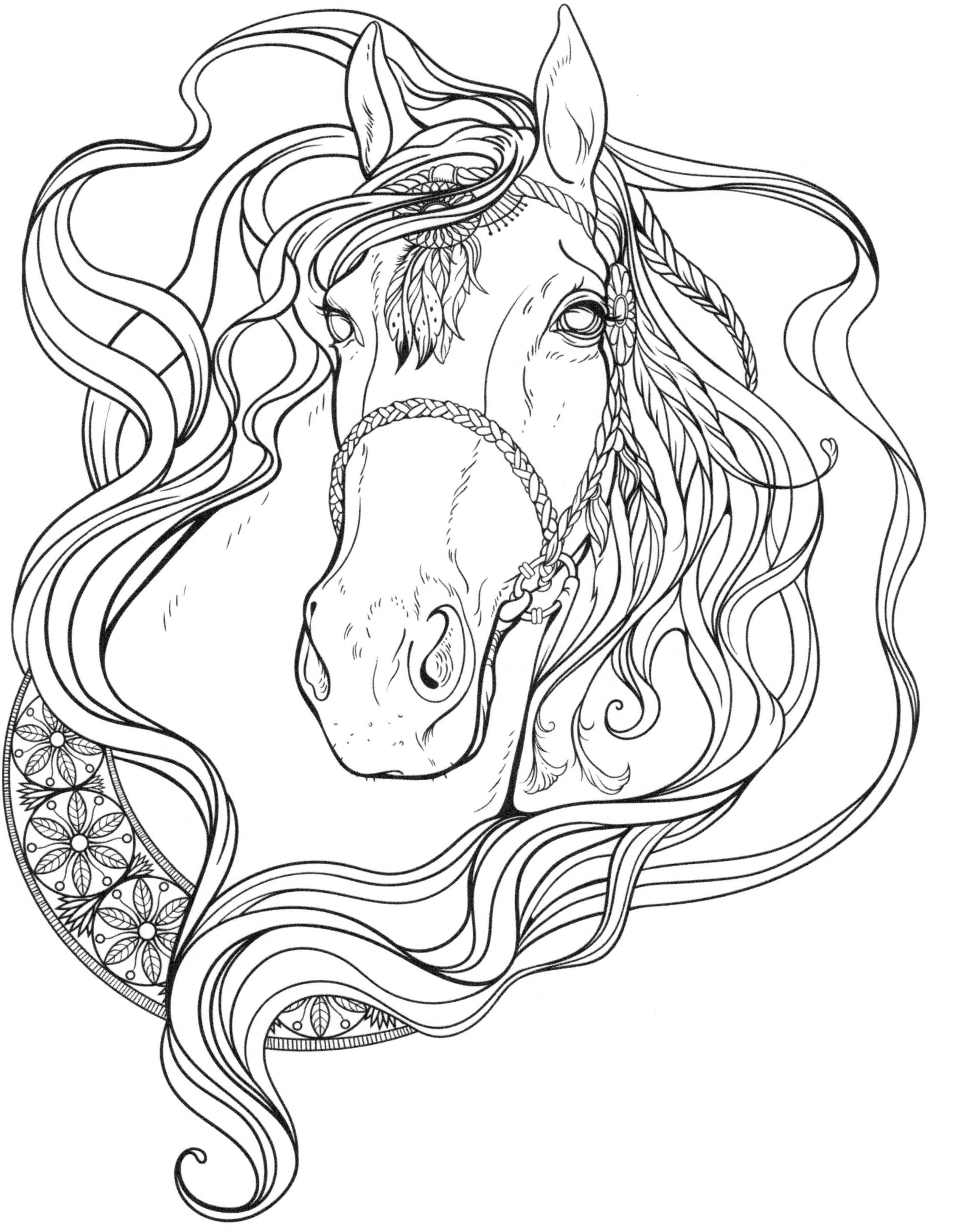

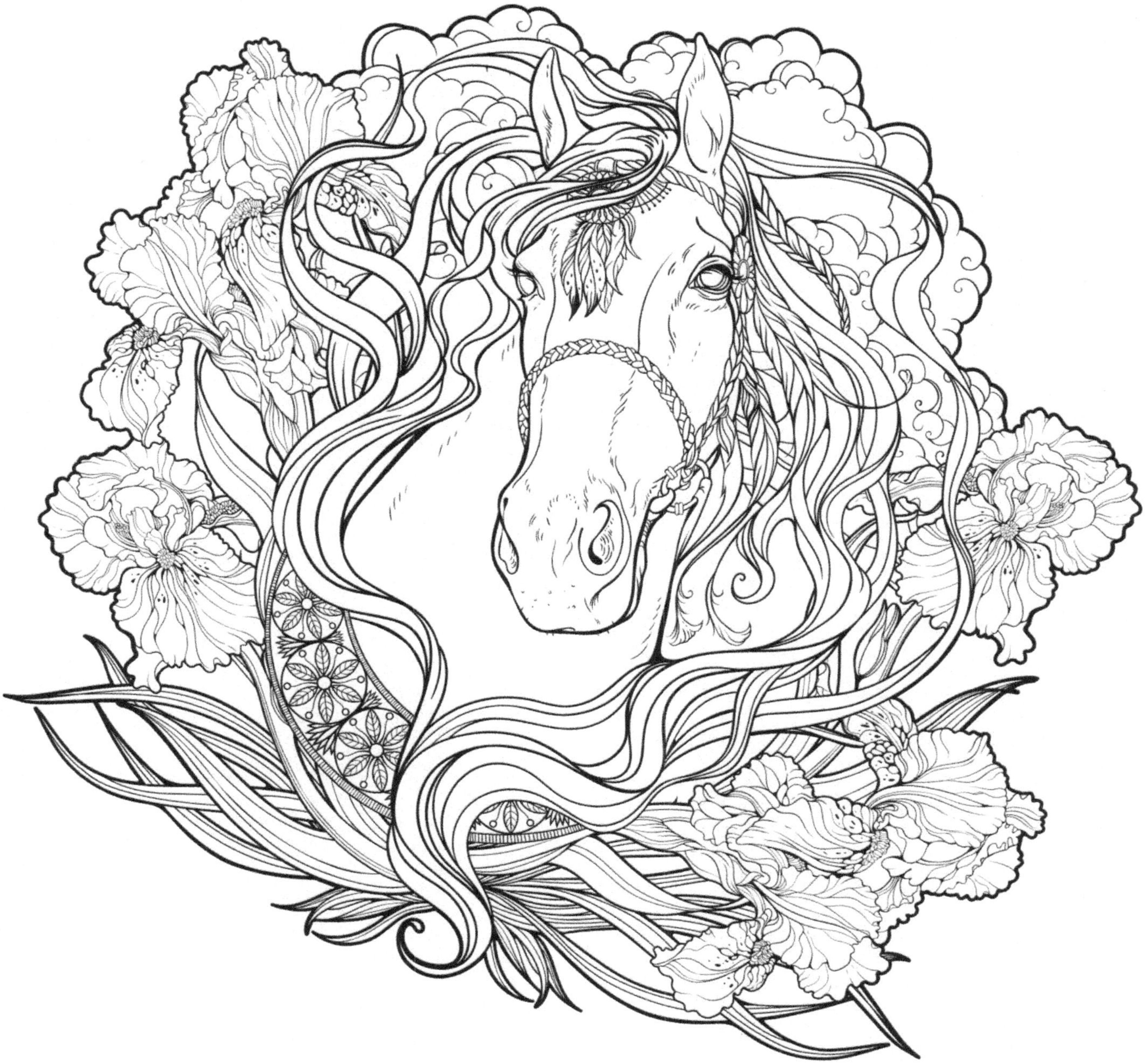

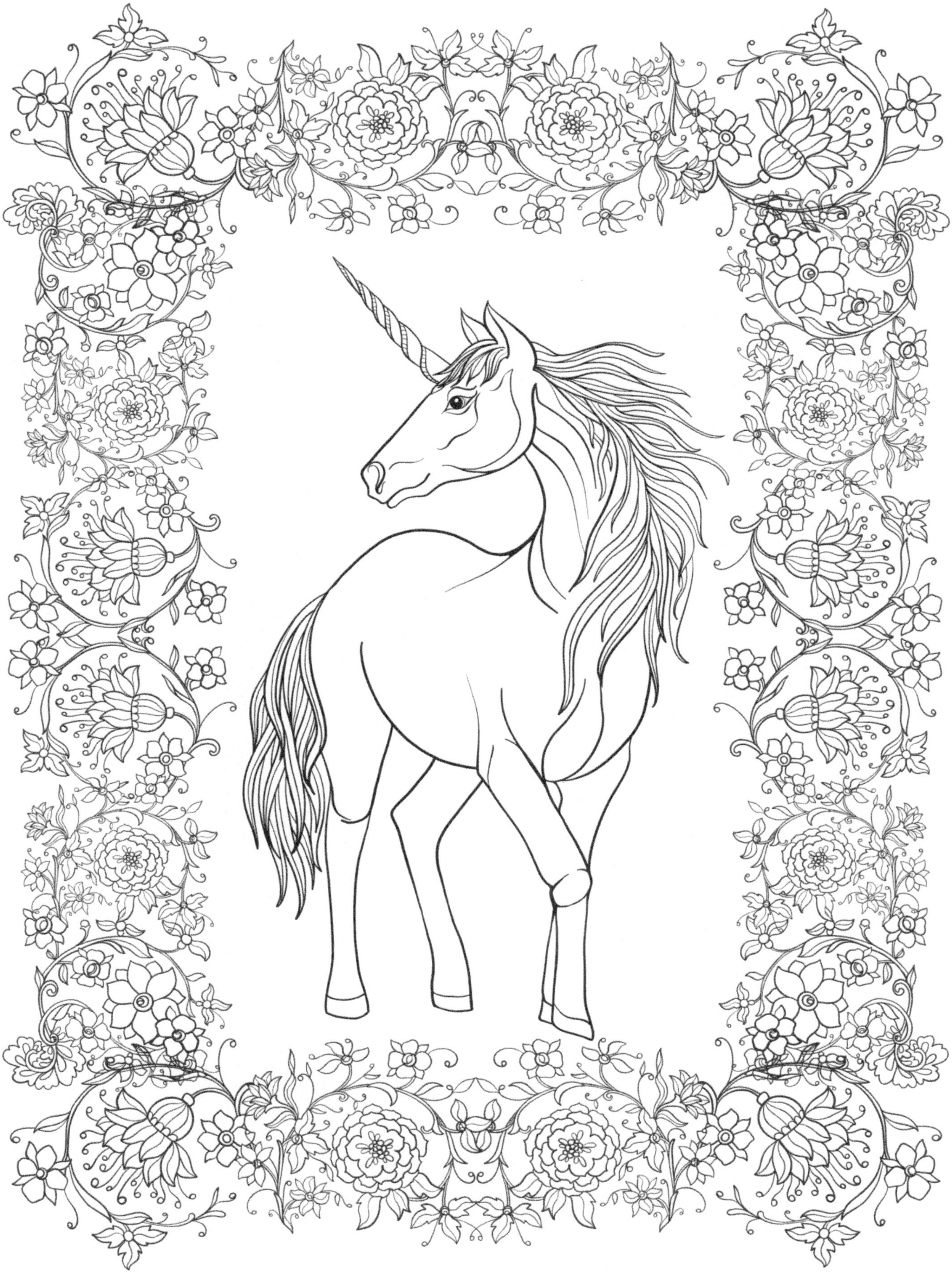

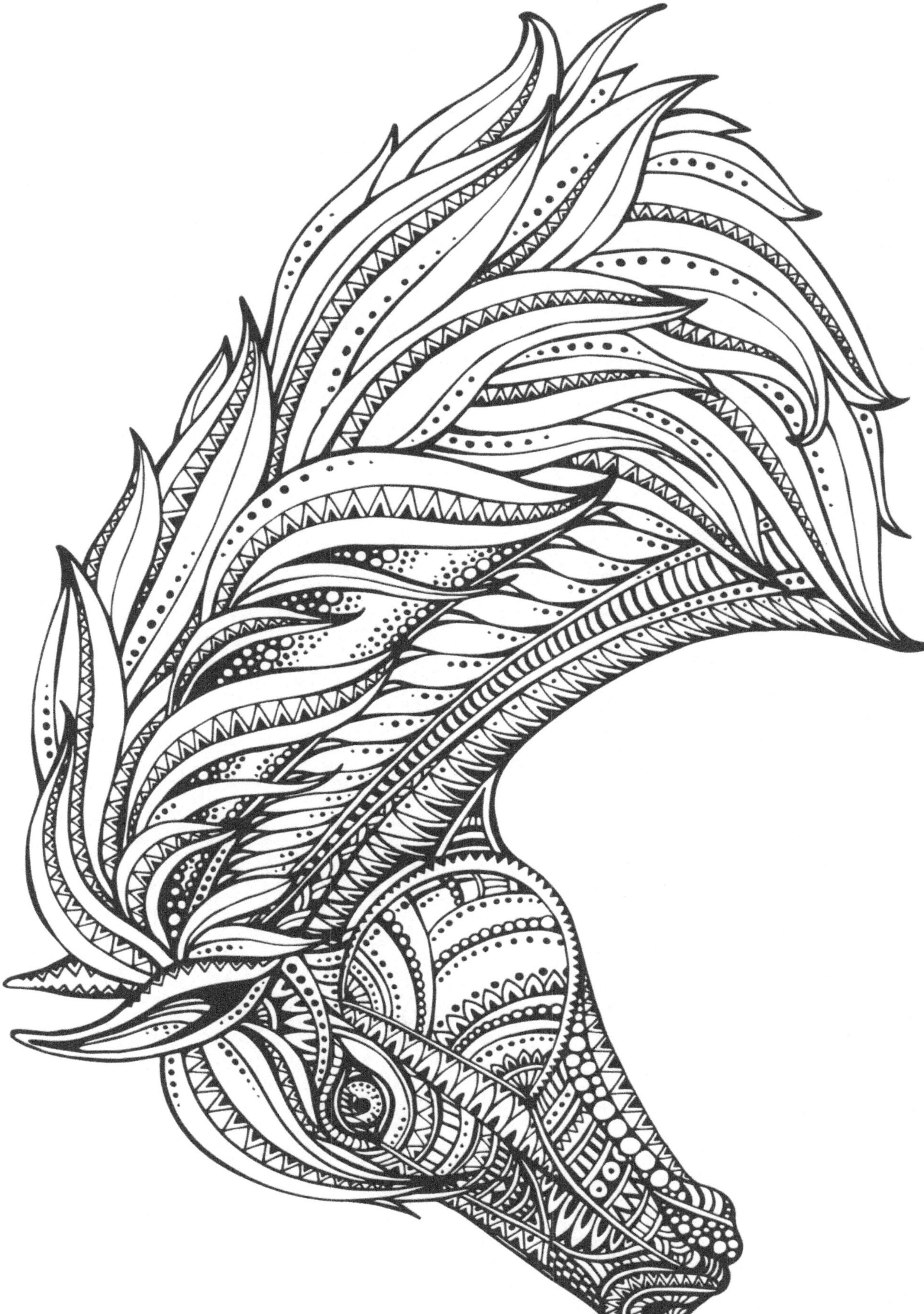

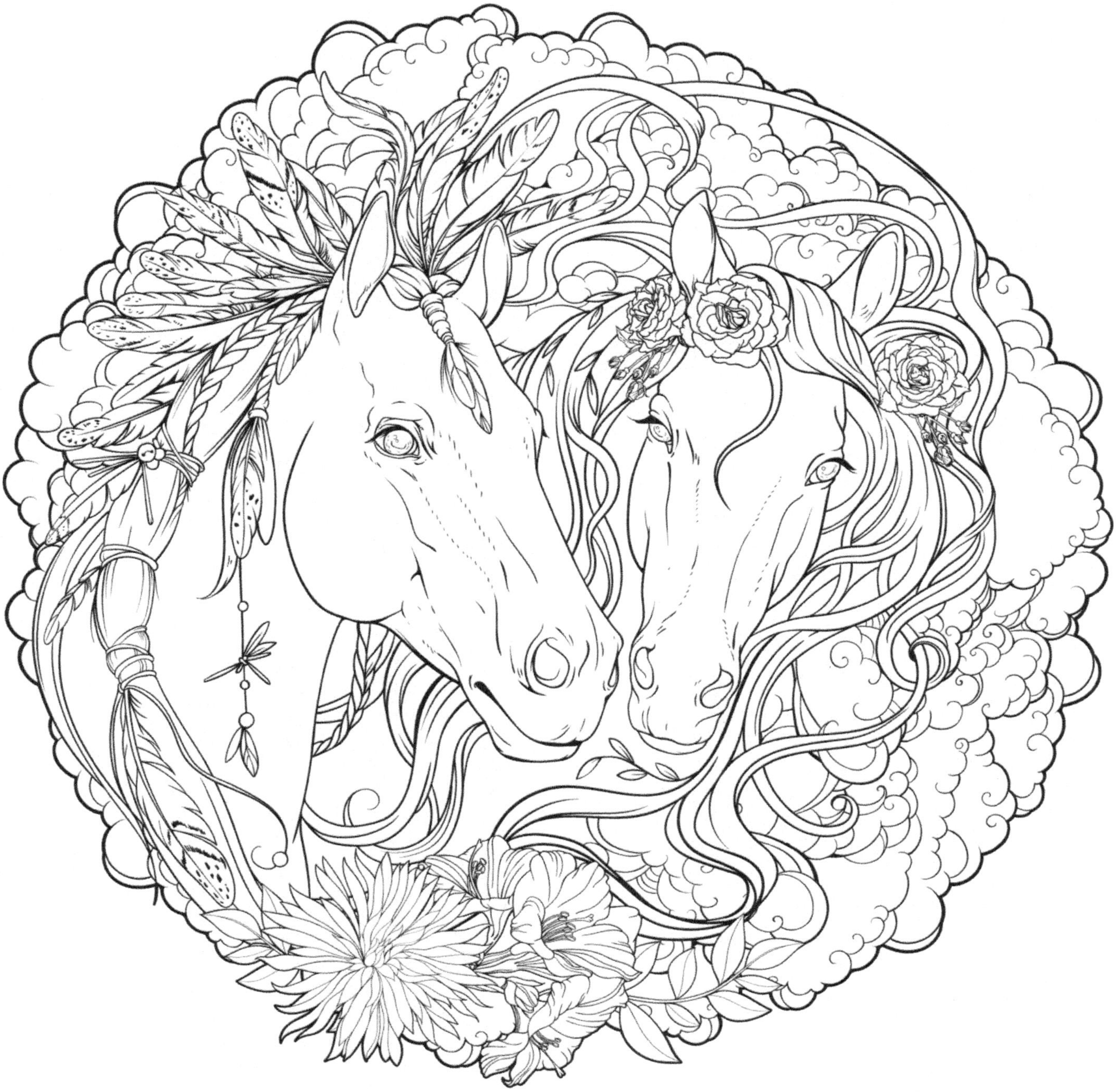

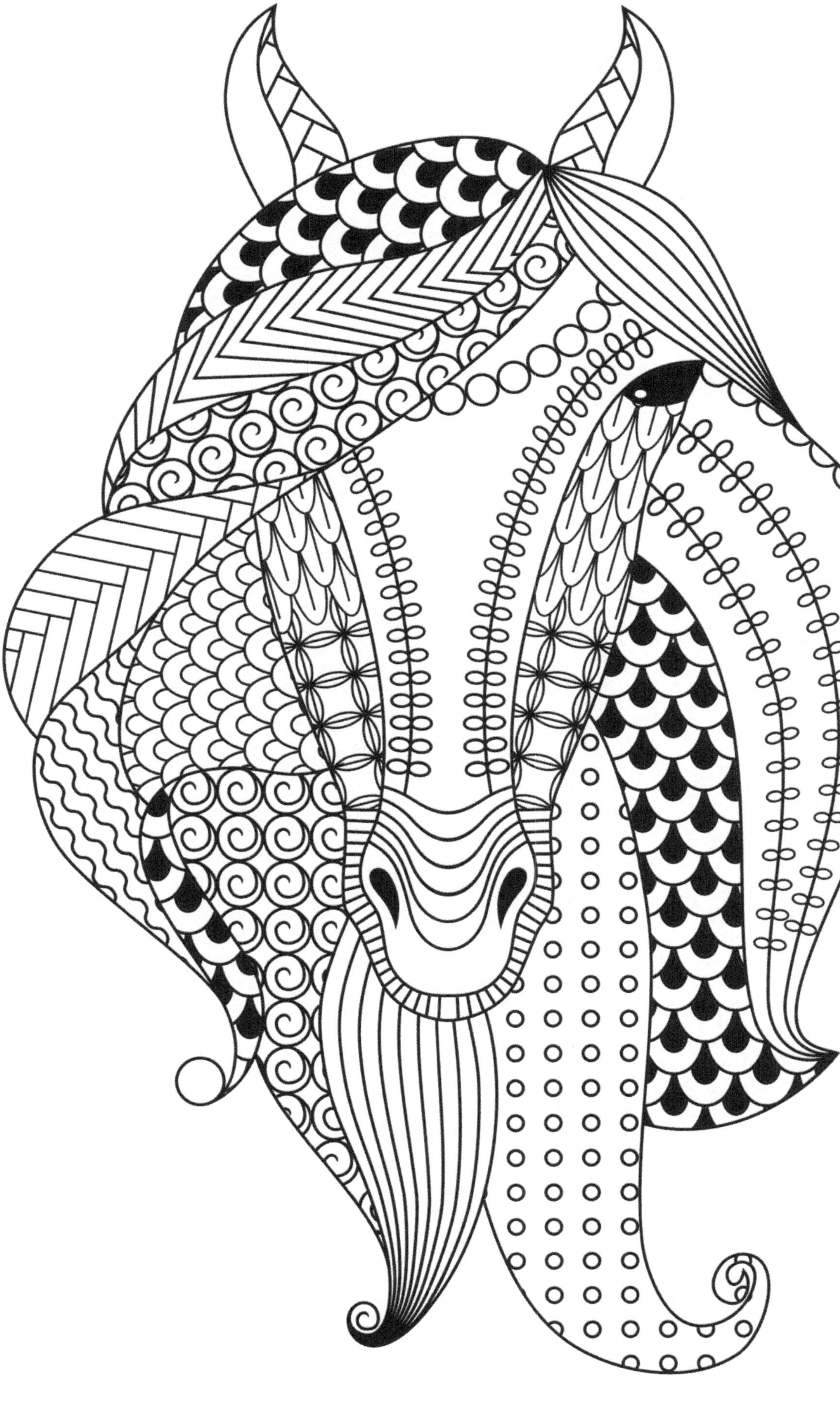

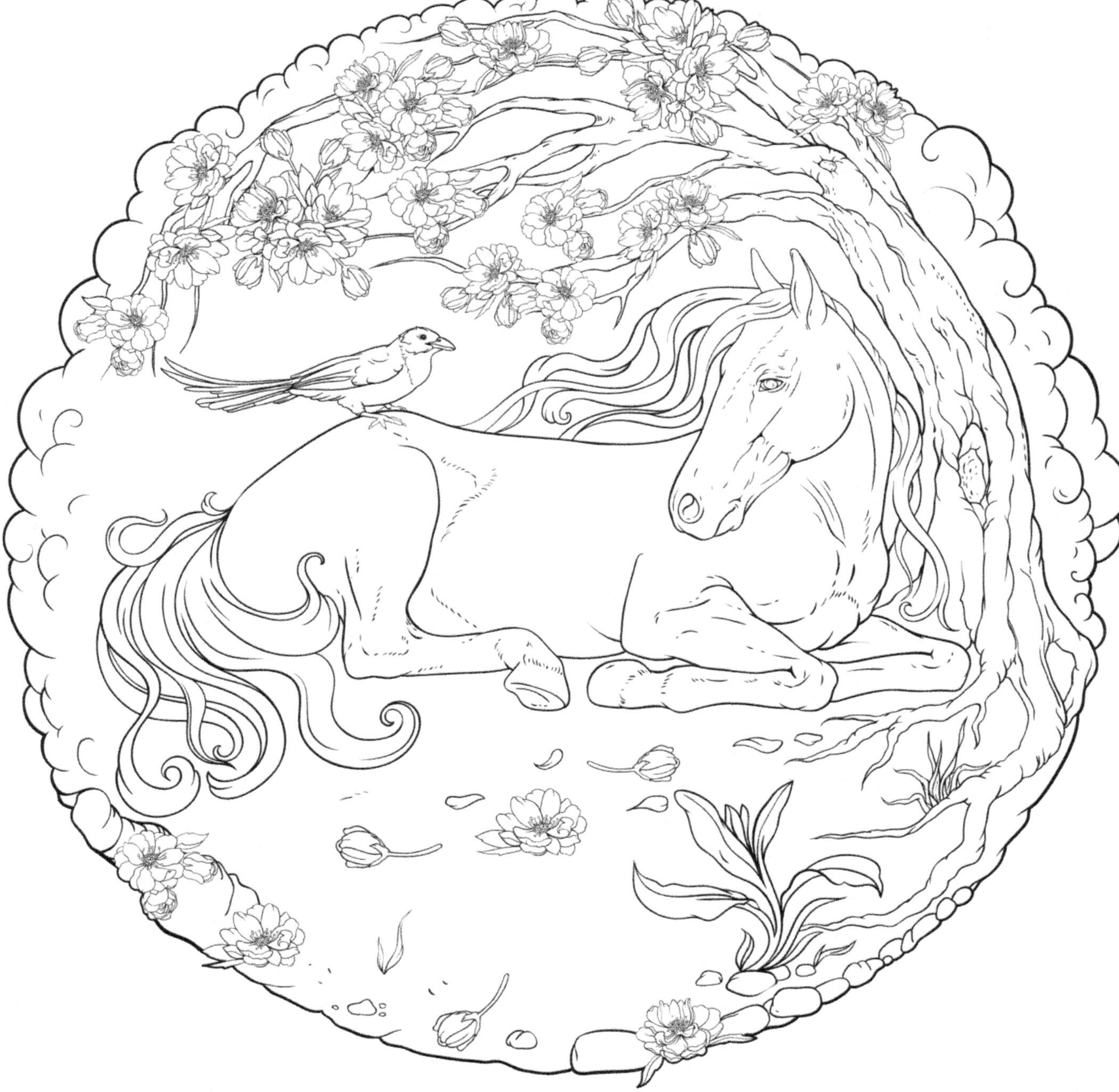

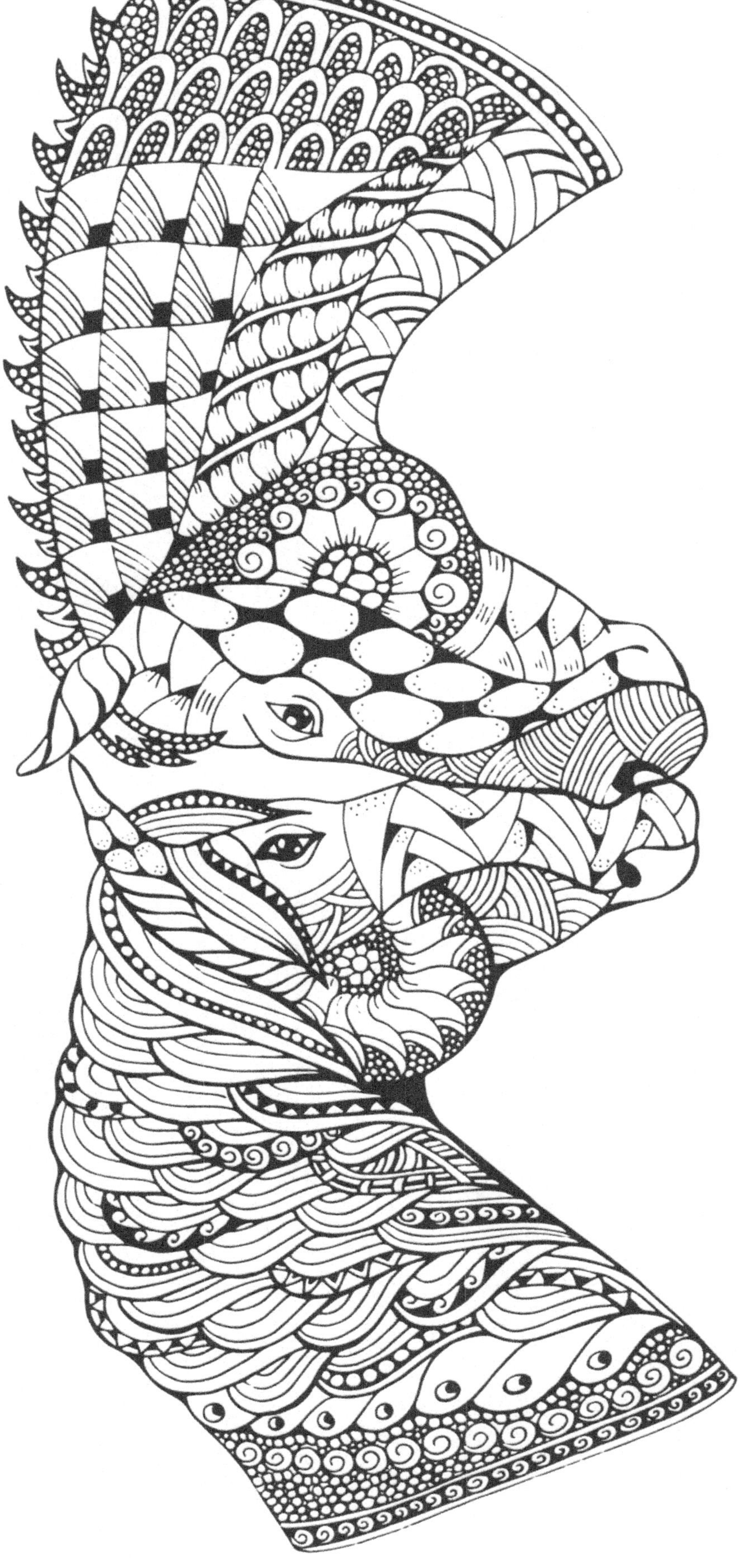

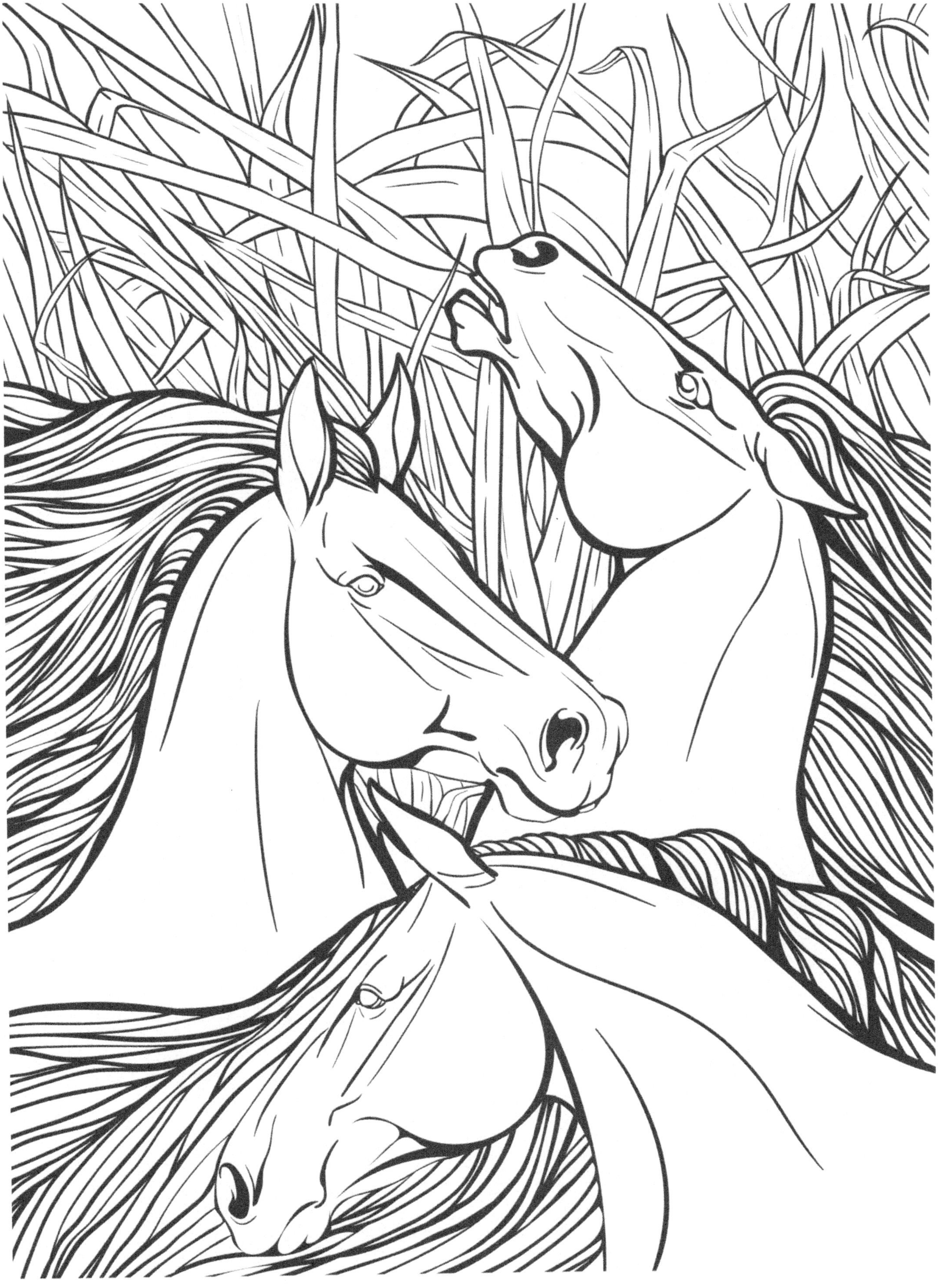

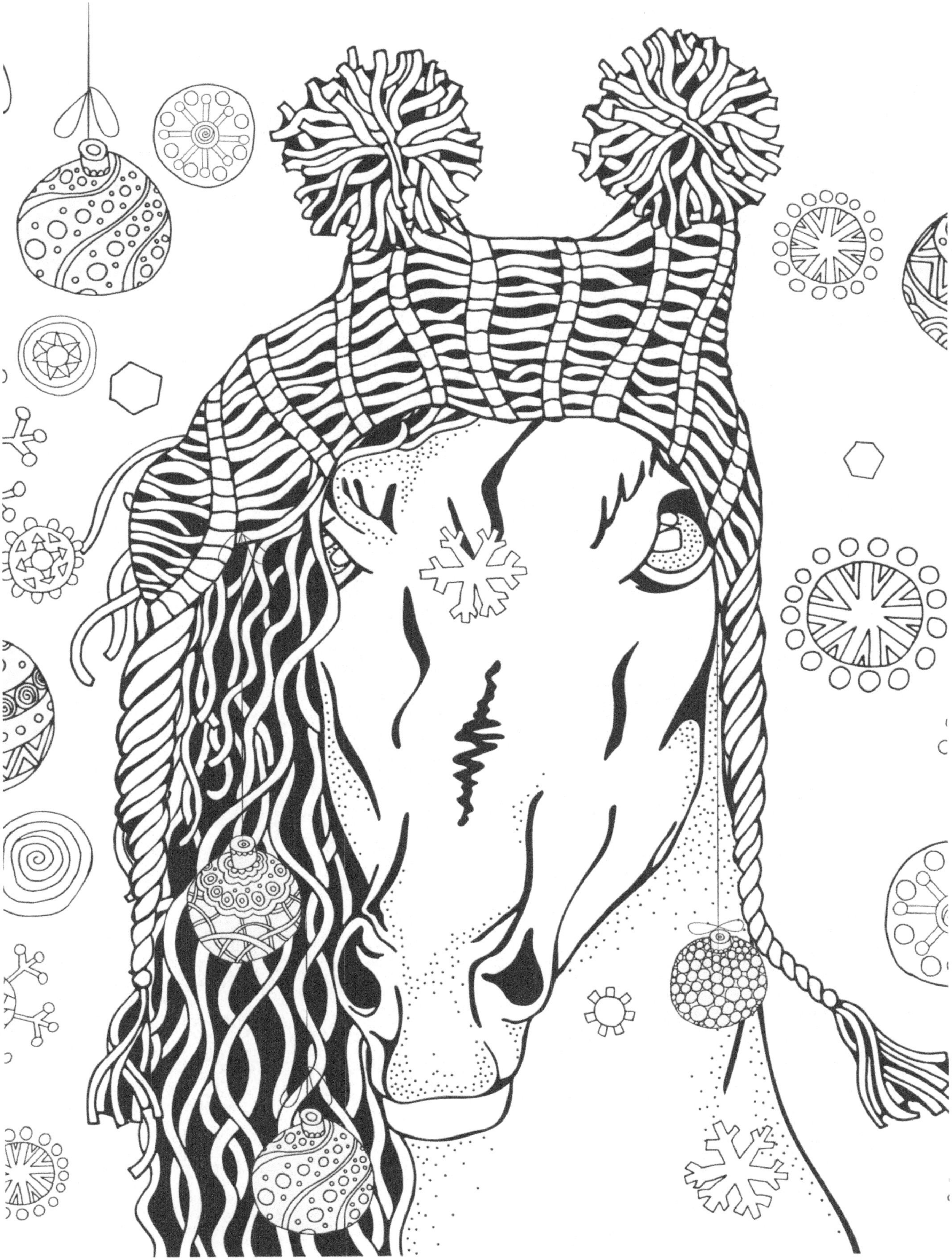

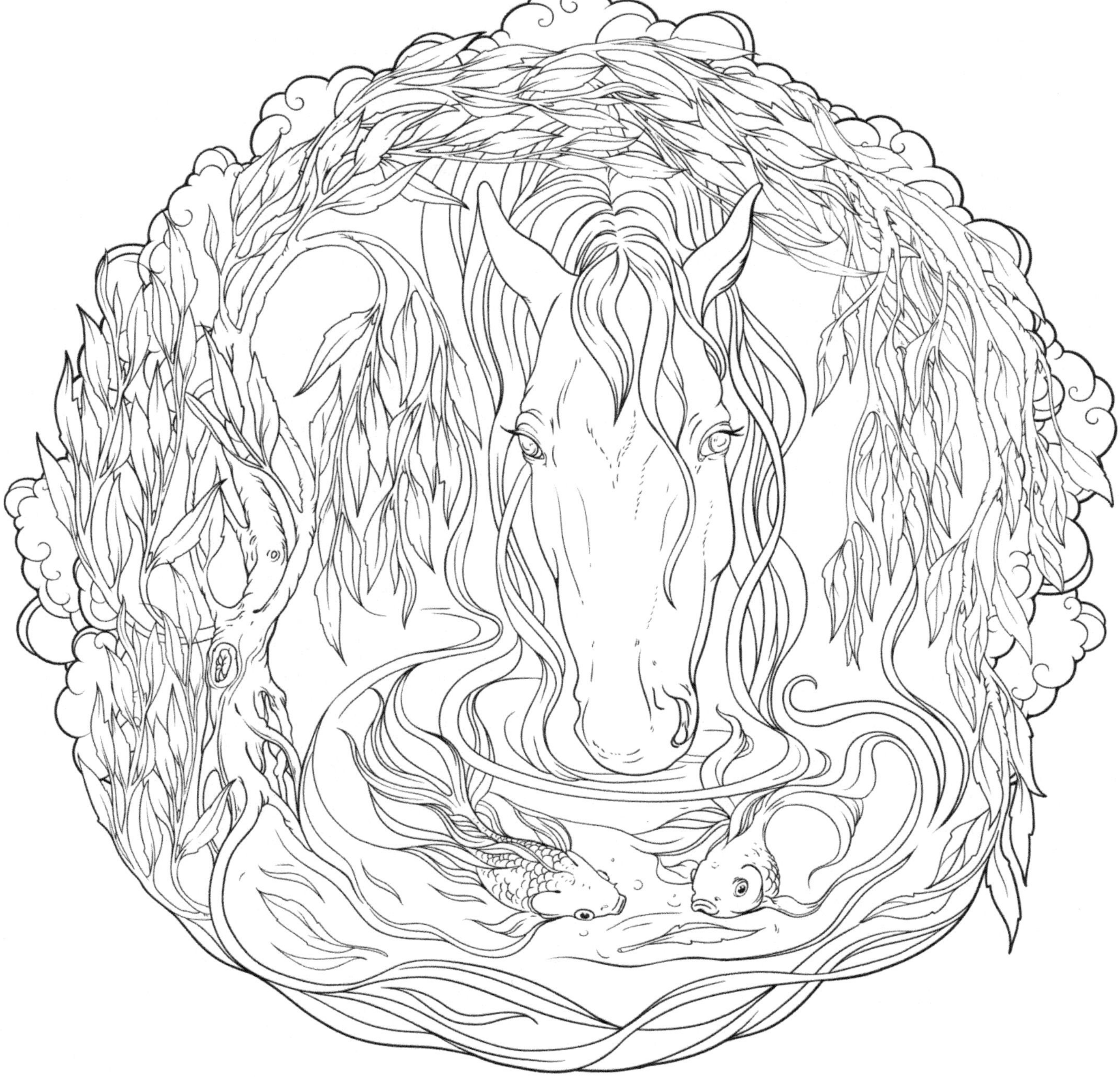

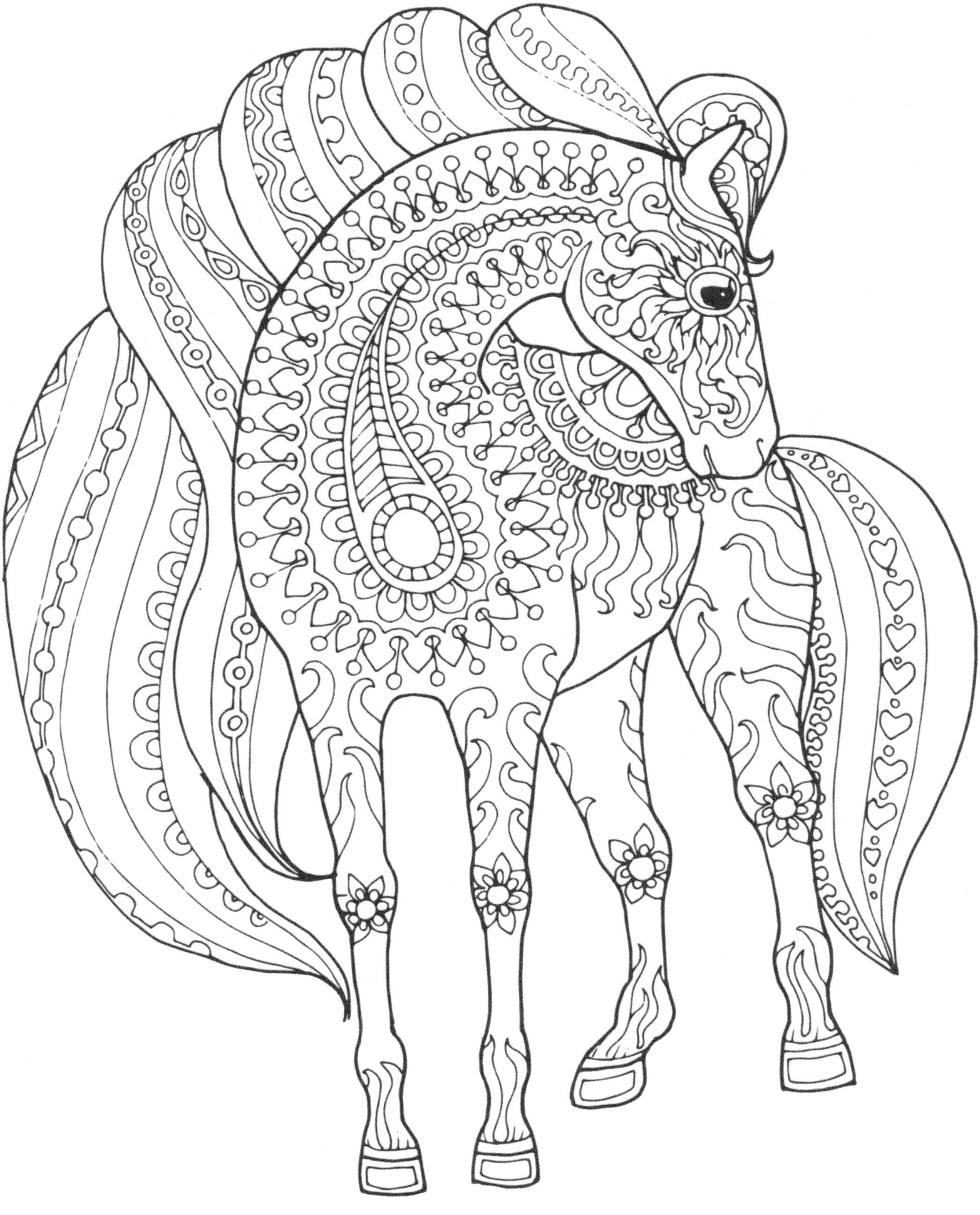

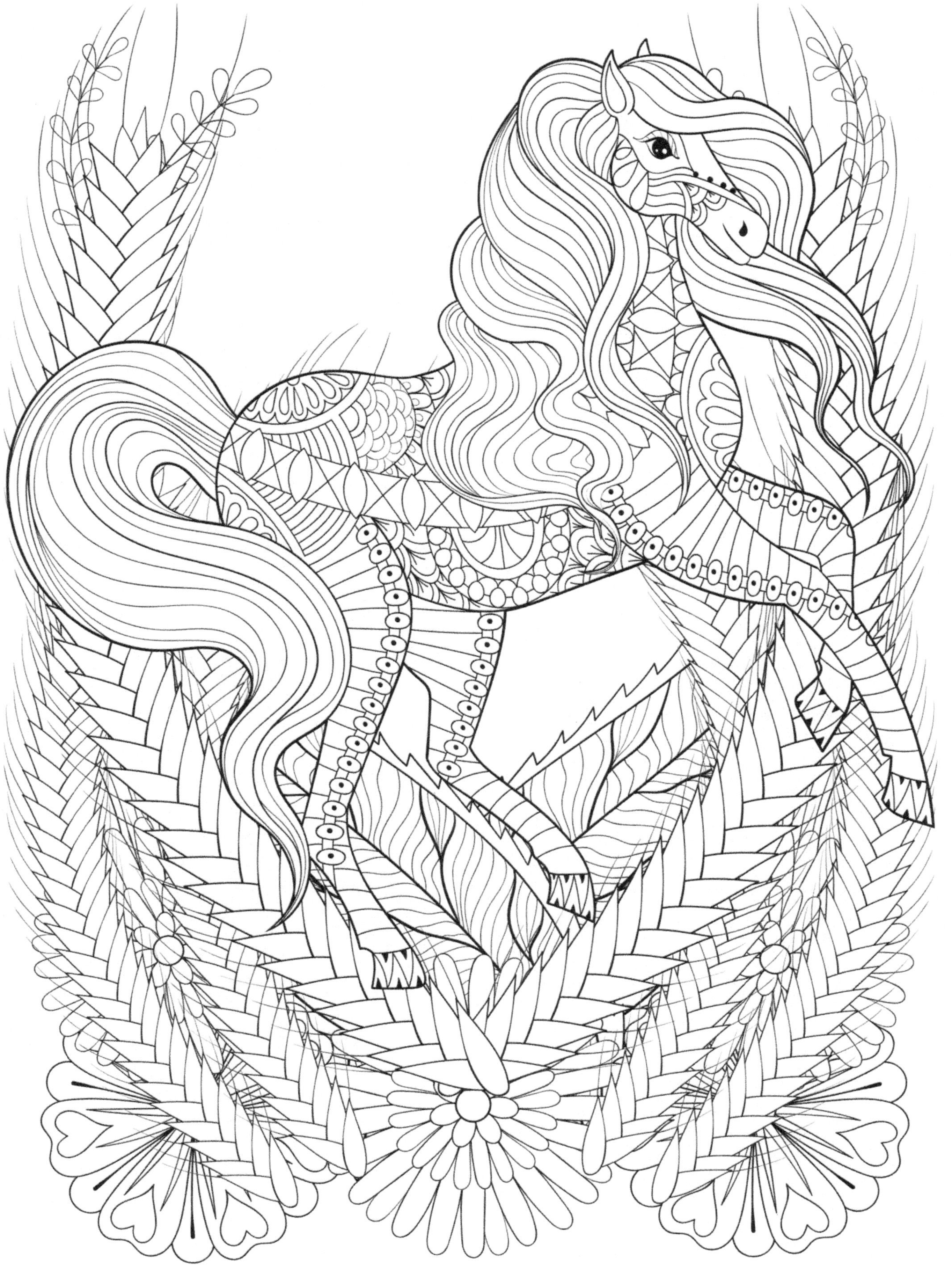

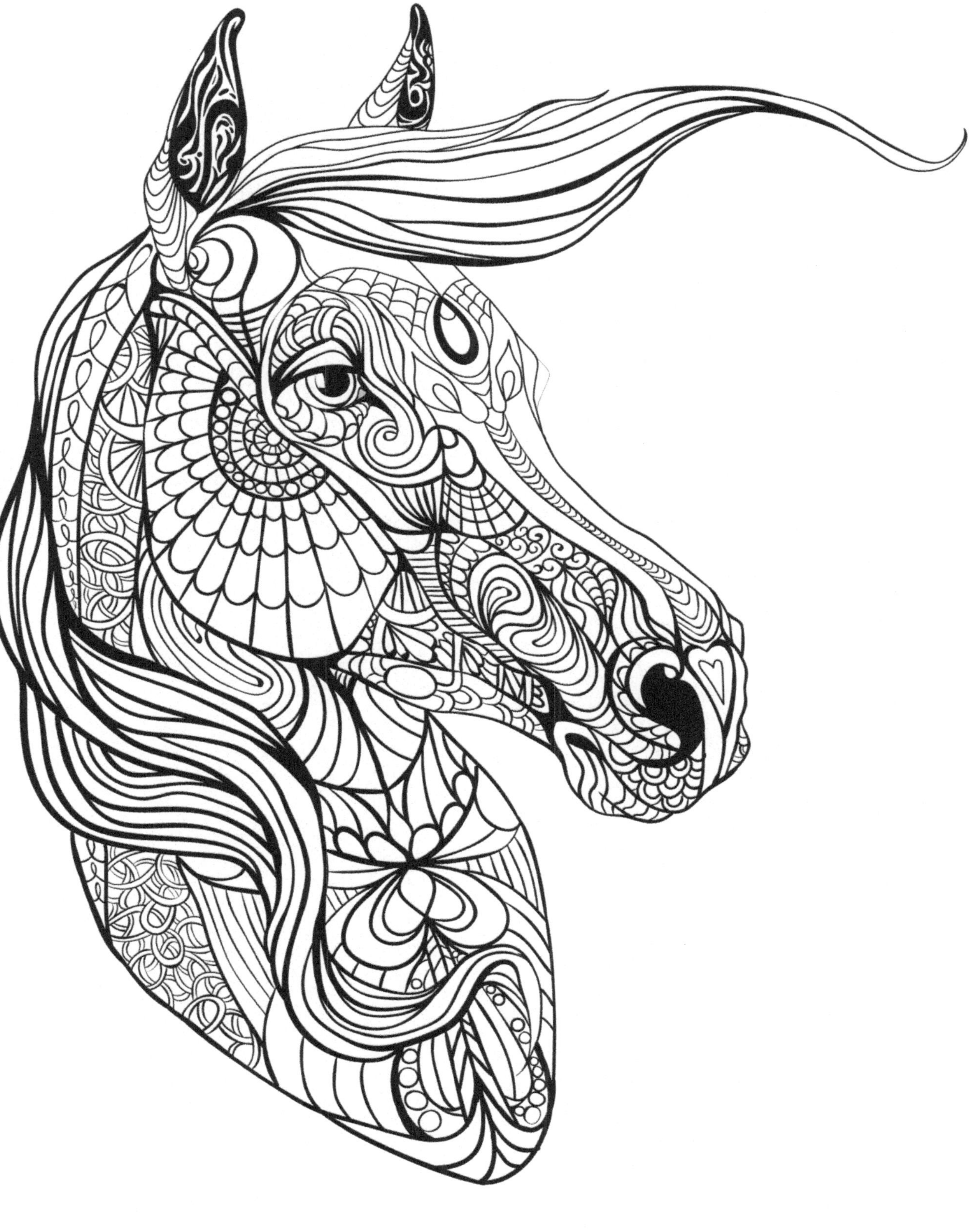

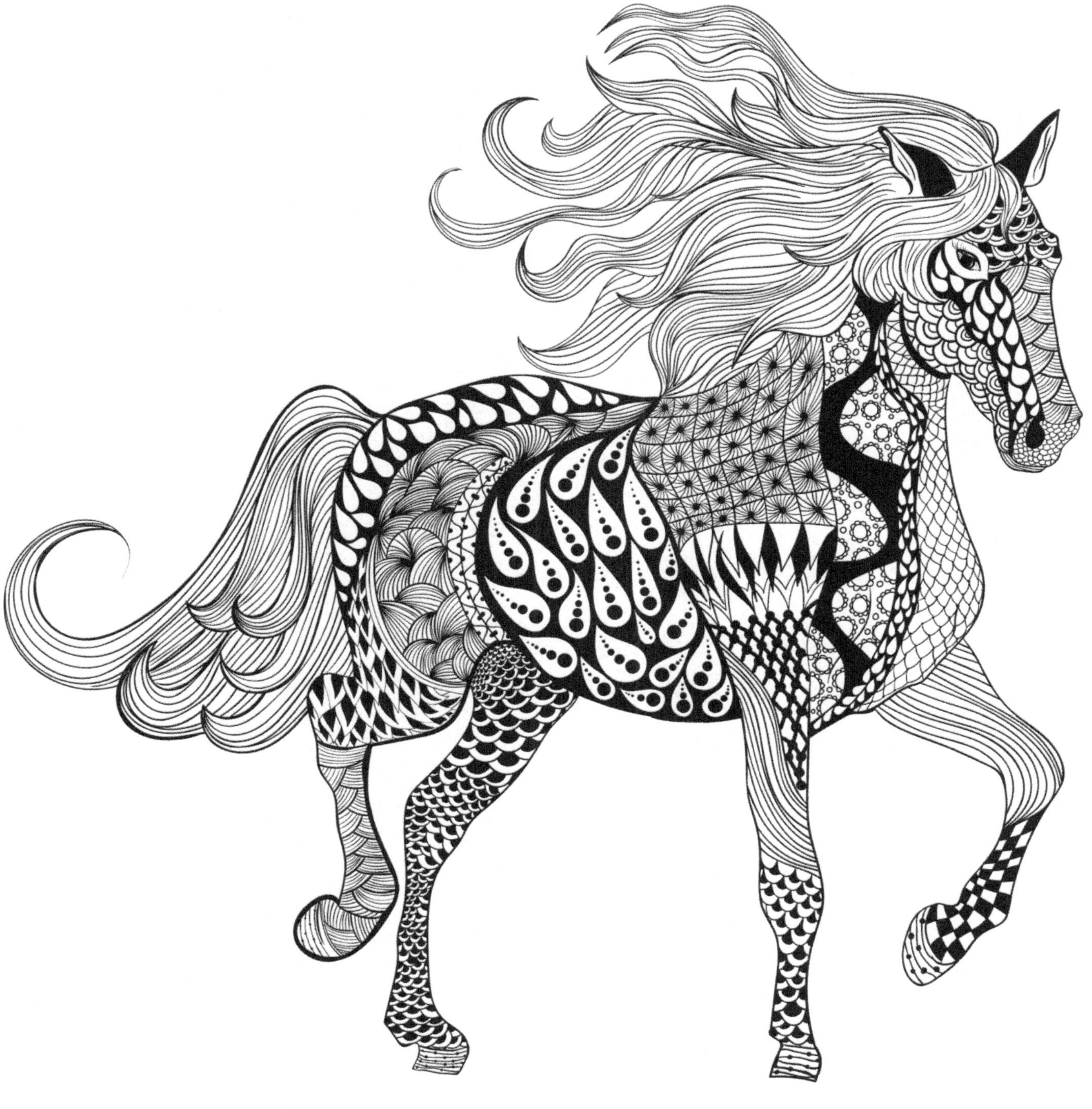

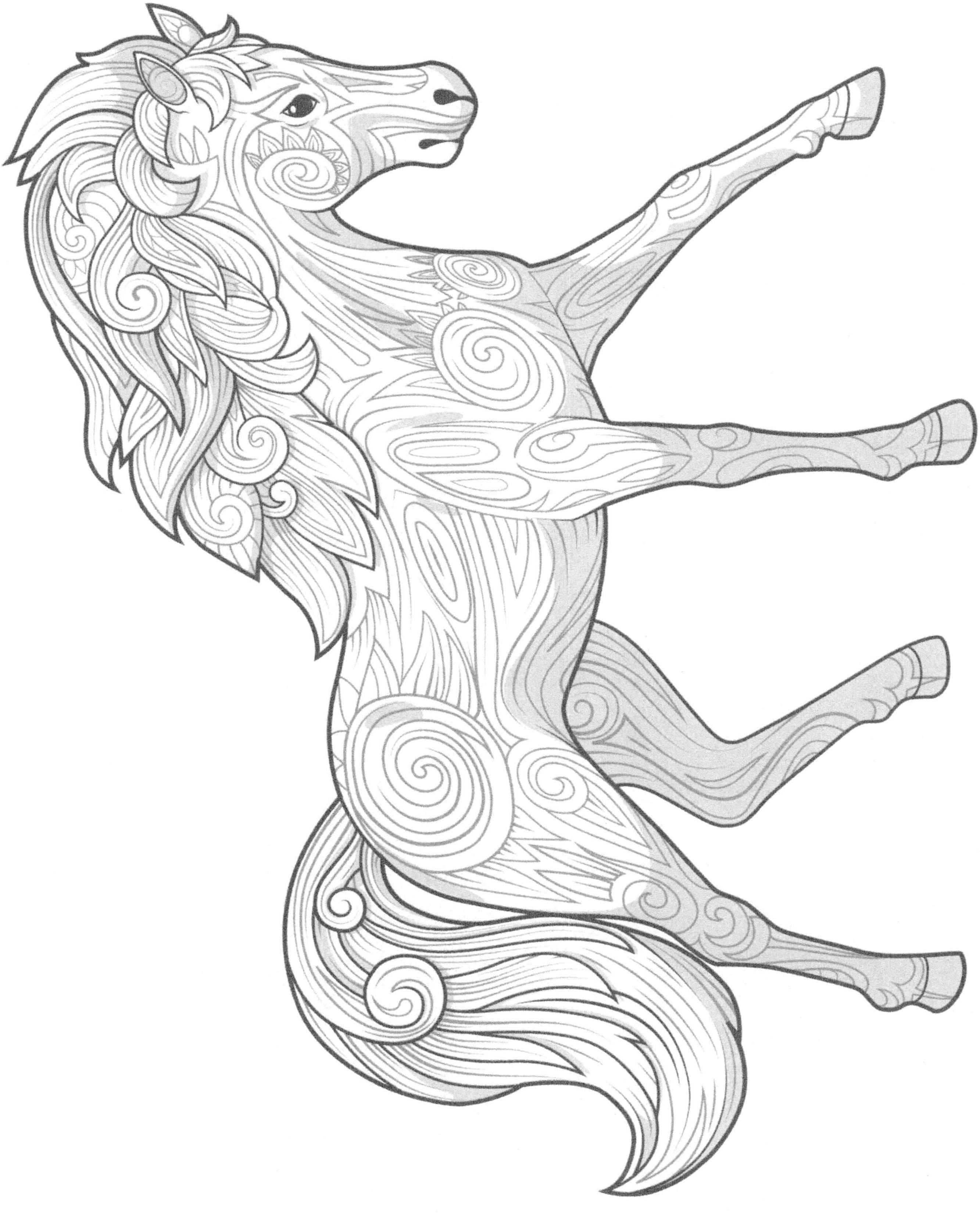

Made in the USA
Monee, IL
29 November 2019

17617606R00037